Give Me a Clue

THEODORE CLYMER
RICHARD L. VENEZKY

Consultants
CLAIRE HENRY
DALE D. JOHNSON
HUGHES MOIR
P. DAVID PEARSON
PHYLLIS WEAVER

Ginn and Company

0-663-38720-5

Acknowledgments: Grateful acknowledgment is made
to the following publishers, authors, and agents for
permission to use and adapt copyrighted material:

Addison-Wesley Publishing Company, Inc., for
"How Mud Was Discovered" and "All About Mud" by
Oliver G. Selfridge. Adapted from *All About Mud,* ©
1978, by Oliver G. Selfridge by permission of Addison-
Wesley Publishing Company, Inc.

Atheneum Publishers, Inc., for the poems
beginning "By the sandy water . . ." and "My great corn
plants . . ." from *Songs of the Dream People: Chants
and Images from the Indians and Eskimos of North
America* edited by James Houston (A Margaret K.
McElderry Book). Copyright © 1972 by James
Houston. Used by permission of Atheneum
Publishers, and of Academic Press Canada.

Coward, McCann & Geoghegan, Inc., for "Wind Is
to Feel" by Shirley Cook Hatch. Adapted by
permission of Coward, McCann & Geoghegan, Inc.
from *Wind Is to Feel* by Shirley Cook Hatch. Copyright
© 1973 by Shirley Cook Hatch. Also for "Nate the Great
and the Lost List," with selected illustrations, by
Marjorie Weinman Sharmat. Adapted by permission of
Coward, McCann & Geoghegan, Inc. from *Nate the
Great and the Lost List* by Marjorie Weinman Sharmat.
Copyright © 1975 by Marjorie Weinman Sharmat.

Crown Publishers, Inc., for "Frederick's Alligator,"
adapted, with selected illustrations, by Esther Allen
Peterson. Taken from *Frederick's Alligator* by Esther
Allen Peterson and Susanna Natti. Text Copyright ©
1979 by Esther A. Peterson. Illustrations Copyright ©
1979 by Susanna Natti. Used by permission of Crown
Publishers, Inc.

Elsevier-Dutton Publishing Co., Inc., for "The
Pickle Plan," adapted from *The Pickle Plan* by Marilyn
Singer. Text copyright © 1978 by Marilyn Singer.
Reprinted by permission of the publisher, E. P. Dutton.
Also for "Puzzle" from *Street Poems* by Robert
Froman. Copyright © 1971 by Robert Froman.
Reprinted by permission of the publisher, E. P. Dutton.

Harper & Row, Publishers, Inc., for selected
illustrations from and an adapted abridgment of the
text of *Corn Is Maize: The Gift of the Indians,* written
and illustrated by Aliki. Copyright © 1976 by Aliki
Brandenberg. A Let's-Read-and-Find-Out Book. By
permission of Thomas Y. Crowell, Publishers. Also for
the abridged, adapted text of *How to Be a Nature
Detective* by Millicent Selsam. Text copyright © 1958,
1963 by Millicent Selsam. By permission of Harper &
Row, Publishers, Inc. Also for "I Have a Sister," a text
excerpt from *I Have a Sister, My Sister Is Deaf* by
Jeanne Whitehouse Peterson, adapted for use as a
poem. Text copyright © 1977 by Jeanne Whitehouse
Peterson. By permission of Harper & Row, Publishers,
Inc.

Holt, Rinehart and Winston, Publishers, for "Fish
Story" with selected illustrations, from *Fish Story* by
Robert Tallon. Copyright © 1977 by Robert Tallon.
Adapted by permission of Holt, Rinehart and Winston,
Publishers.

Little, Brown and Company for the poem "Tooth
Trouble" from *Take Sky* by David McCord. Copyright
© 1961, 1962 by David McCord. By permission of Little,
Brown and Company.

Macmillan Publishing Co., Inc., for "The Turnip"
by Janina Domanska. Adapted with permission of
Macmillan Publishing Co., Inc. from *The Turnip* by
Janina Domanska. Copyright © 1972 by Janina
Domanska.

G. P. Putnam's Sons for "The Wobbly Tooth" by
Nancy Evans Cooney. Adapted by permission of G. P.
Putnam's Sons from *The Wobbly Tooth* by Nancy
Evans Cooney. Copyright © 1978 by Nancy Evans
Cooney. Also for "Kumi and the Pearl" by Patricia
Miles Martin. Adapted by permission of G. P. Putnam's
Sons from *Kumi and the Pearl* by Patricia Miles Martin.
Copyright © 1968 by Patricia Miles Martin.

Random House, Inc., for "The Surprise Party"
(Parts 1 and 2) by Annabelle Prager. Text adapted by
permission of Pantheon Books, a Division of Random
House, Inc. from *The Surprise Party*, by Annabelle
Prager. Copyright © 1977 by Annabelle Prager.

Charles Scribner's Sons for the poem "Written in
Sand," an excerpt from *We Walk in Sandy Places* by
Byrd Baylor. Text copyright © 1976 by Byrd Baylor.
Reprinted by permission of Charles Scribner's Sons.

Franklin Watts, Inc., for "Kate's Secret Riddle
Book," adapted from *Kate's Secret Riddle Book* by Sid
Fleischman. Text copyright © 1977 by Albert S.
Fleischman. Used by permission of Franklin Watts, Inc.

Abelard-Schuman Limited, London, for "Puzzle"
from *Street Poems* by Robert Froman. Reprinted by
permission of the British publisher.

Bret Adams Limited for "Pea Soup and Sea
Serpents," adapted from *Pea Soup and Sea Serpents*
by William E. Schroder. Copyright © 1977 by William E.
Schroder. Used by permission of the author's agent.

Curtis Brown, Ltd., New York, for "Kate's Secret
Riddle Book," adapted from *Kate's Secret Riddle Book*
by Sid Fleischman. Reprinted by permission of Curtis
Brown, Ltd. Text Copyright © 1977 by Albert S.
Fleischman.

Down East Books, Camden, Maine, for "Andre: A
Very Special Seal" by Suzanne Higgins, based on *The
Story of Andre* by Lew Dietz. Copyright 1979 by Lew
(Continued on page 286)

Contents

Unit 1 SPECIAL PEOPLE, SPECIAL TIMES

4

Unit 4 DON'T SNEEZE NOW 184

Book-length Story

Special Peop

People are special. Each of us does something special every day. We talk and listen. We play and help. We do special things for other people, too.

The people in this unit are waiting to share something special. Nicky plans a birthday party for . . . himself. Ana and Felipe share an idea. They take time to make a special gift. Jenny has a special pet to talk about. Will her friends listen to her? Frederick thinks his alligator is special.

Special people are waiting to meet *you*. Come and spend some time with them.

le, Times

Special

9

The Wobbly Tooth

Nancy Evans Cooney

Elizabeth Ann had a wobbly tooth. This wobbly tooth was different. This tooth wouldn't come out.

Elizabeth Ann's mother said not to worry. "That tooth just isn't ready to come out."

But Elizabeth Ann did worry. She kept thinking about that wobbly tooth. She decided to get rid of it.

She tried pulling the tooth out with her fingers. It wouldn't come out.

She tried jumping up and down. It wouldn't come out.

She tried turning cartwheels. It wouldn't come out.

Elizabeth Ann sat sadly on her steps. She had run out of ideas.

Maybe her mother was right. She shouldn't worry. That tooth just wasn't ready to come out.

So Elizabeth Ann decided to forget all about that old wobbly tooth.

She took her best book about dogs and started to read. But her tongue didn't forget that wobbly tooth. Her tongue kept sneaking over to it. She sadly put the book away.

Jane came over to ask Elizabeth Ann to play baseball. Elizabeth Ann smiled and said, "Great!" She decided she would play. She liked playing baseball with her friends. She liked the crack of the ball on the bat. She liked the sound that said she had made a good catch.

It was a hard game. First one team got a run. Then the other team did.

Elizabeth Ann worked hard trying to help her team. She forgot all about forgetting.

In the first inning, Elizabeth Ann just missed catching a ball. In the next inning, she hit a fly ball right to another player.

By the last inning, her team was still behind by one run. She had to get a run and tie the game!

Elizabeth Ann stepped up to the plate.

The first ball went by before she could move. When the next ball came, she was ready.

CRACK went the ball when she hit it. It went by first base. So did Elizabeth Ann.

On the ball flew. On ran Elizabeth Ann.

She reached second base and then third. She headed for home plate.

Elizabeth Ann saw the ball coming. She kept going faster and faster. At last she slid into home plate. But the ball got there first. She was out!

Elizabeth Ann sat panting and dusty. She was feeling very sad. What a day! Nothing seemed to go right.

She smiled sadly at her friends. "I tried," she said.

Jane cried, "Look!"

Elizabeth Ann looked at everyone. They were looking at her.

"Elizabeth Ann has lost a tooth!" Jane cried.

Elizabeth Ann's tongue went over to feel her tooth. There was nothing but a hole. That wobbly tooth was gone!

Elizabeth Ann smiled. It must have been ready to come out at last.

Tooth Trouble

When I see the dentist
I take him all my teeth:
Some of me's above them,
But most of me's beneath.

And one is in my pocket,
Because it grew so loose
That I could fit a string to it
And tighten up the noose.

I'll grow another, dentist says,
And shall not need to noose it.
Another still to drill and fill?
Not me! I won't produce it.

David McCord

The Surprise Party
Part 1   Annabelle Prager

"Know what?" said Nicky.

"No, what?" said Albert.

"My birthday is coming," said Nicky. "I am going to have a birthday party."

"Great!" said Albert. "I love birthday parties!"

"Come on. I need you to help me," said Nicky.

Nicky took out his bank. He shook it upside down. Out fell two coins.

"Oh, no," he said. "This isn't enough for a party."

"What are you going to do?" asked Albert.

"I'll think of something," said Nicky. Then he smiled.

"I know," he said. "I'll have a surprise party."

"A surprise party for who?" asked Albert.

"A surprise party for me," said Nicky.

"You can't give a surprise party for yourself," said Albert. "You won't be surprised."

"I know I can't give a surprise party for myself," said Nicky. "But YOU can. You and Ann, and Jenny and Jan, and Morris and Doris, and Dan can give the party."

"How are we going to do that?" asked Albert.

"Easy," said Nicky. "You'll say—*Nicky's birthday is coming. Let's give him a surprise party.* Then they'll say—*What a good idea. We love surprise parties. You can bring the cake. Ann can bring the paper plates.*"

"Oh, I get it," said Albert. "Everyone will bring something for the party. What a good idea."

"You can get the party ready at my house while I am out having my tuba lesson," Nicky said. "When I come home, you will yell SURPRISE! I'll be surprised if this isn't the best surprise party ever."

Albert ran home. He called up Ann, and
Jenny and Jan, and Morris and Doris, and Dan.
Sure enough, they all said, "What a good idea!
We love surprise parties."

They all met at Albert's house to plan the
party.

"We can fix the party at Nicky's house
while he is out having his tuba lesson," Albert
said. "When he comes home, we will yell
SURPRISE!"

Just then the telephone rang. Albert answered it. "Hello," he said.

It was Nicky. "I forgot to tell you something," said Nicky. "I love balloons with Happy Birthday on them."

"OK," said Albert. "Good-by."

"Who was that?" asked Ann.

Albert thought very fast. "That was my Aunt Betsy," he said. "Shall we have balloons with Happy Birthday on them?"

"Yes, yes, yes," shouted everyone.

23

The telephone rang again. Albert answered it. It was Nicky again.

"I forgot to ask," said Nicky. "Are we having snappers? The kind that go bang when you pull them?"

"Sure, Aunt Betsy," said Albert.

He slammed down the telephone. Then he turned to the others. "Shall we have snappers?" he asked.

"Do you mean the kind that go bang when you pull them?" asked Jenny. "I love them."

The telephone rang again.

"Let me answer it," said Jan.

"No, no, no," cried Albert, grabbing the telephone. It was Nicky again.

"I forgot to tell you," said Nicky. "I love the color blue."

" Oh, yes, Aunt Betsy, " said Albert. "GOOD-BY!"

"Why does your aunt call you all the time?" asked Morris and Doris.

" My Aunt Betsy likes me, " said Albert. "Now let me think. Nicky loves the color blue. Shall I make a beautiful blue birthday cake?"

" Oh, yes ! Will Nicky be surprised ! " everyone said.

The Surprise Party
Part 2

The next day Nicky and Albert were out for a walk.

"It wouldn't be good if the others found out that I know about the party!" said Nicky.

"Quiet," said Albert. "Here comes Ann."

"I'll make sure that Ann doesn't think I know about the party," said Nicky.

"Hello," said Ann.

"Hello, Ann," said Nicky. "Guess what I am doing on my birthday."

"What?" asked Ann.

"My tuba teacher is taking me to a concert," said Nicky.

"Oh, NO," said Ann.

"Why do you say *Oh, NO?*" asked Nicky.

"What I wanted to say," said Ann, "was, *Oh, no kidding?* Well, now I have to go see Jenny and Jan, and Morris and Doris, and Dan. Good-by."

Nicky laughed and laughed. "I fooled her," he said. "Now nobody can think that I know about the party. Oh, I can't wait for my birthday to come."

Nicky was walking home from his tuba lesson. He gave a little hop. His birthday had come at last. When Nicky got to his house, it was all dark. He practiced making a surprised face. He opened his front door. Nothing happened.

He went into the front room. Nothing happened. He turned on the light. Nobody was there.

"Where's the party?" he asked himself. "They must be hiding." Nicky waited and waited. Nothing happened.

Then the doorbell rang.

"There they are!" Nicky thought. He practiced making surprised faces on the way to the door.

It was Albert, all by himself.

"Where is my party?" asked Nicky.

"Oh, Nicky," said Albert. "It's too bad. Ann told everyone that you were going to a concert with your tuba teacher. They called off the party."

"Oh, why did I play a trick on my friends?" cried Nicky.

"Don't be too sad," said Albert. "They decided to have the party on your next birthday. You can think about it for a whole year. But I made a cake for you anyway. It's at my house."

29

They walked to Albert's house. Albert opened his front door. Nicky went in. Albert turned on the light.

"SURPRISE! SURPRISE!" shouted Ann, and Jenny and Jan, and Morris and Doris, and Dan.

Nicky looked all around him. There were balloons with Happy Birthday on them. There was a beautiful blue birthday cake. By each blue paper plate, there was a blue snapper. Best of all, there was a big pile of presents. Each one had a surprise inside.

"WOW!" said Nicky.

"Know what?" said Albert.

"No, what?" said Nicky.

" You said you wanted the best surprise party that ever was. So we made it a real surprise."

31

LIFE SKILL: Invitations

In the last story, Nicky tried to plan his surprise party. He wanted everything to be just right. It would have been easier to give the party himself!

Have you ever planned a party? Have you ever been asked to a party? If you have, you may have seen an invitation like the one on the next page.

An invitation must tell at least four things:

1. *Who* is giving the party.
2. *Where* the party is going to be.
3. *When* the party is going to be. This means both the date and the time.
4. *What kind* of party is being held. The party could be a surprise party. It could be a picnic lunch to celebrate spring.

YOU ARE INVITED

TO _A Surprise Birthday Party_

FOR _Nicky_

GIVEN BY _Albert_

PLACE _Albert's House, 8 Special St._

DATE _Saturday, May 20_

TIME _2 P.M._

R.S.V.P. _Albert 555-1234_

Sometimes, an invitation will have the letters _R.S.V.P._ at the end. Next to these letters may be a telephone number. The letters _R.S.V.P._ mean "please answer." They tell you that the person sending the invitation wants to know if you can come. The telephone number is the one to call with your answer.

Pretend you are giving a party. Write out an invitation you would send to a friend. Be sure to tell _who, where, when,_ and _what kind_!

Something Special

Alex Cervantes and E. De Michael Cervantes

It was Grandfather's birthday. Ana had a gift for Grandfather. But she wanted to give him something more. She wanted to give him something special.

"I wish I could think of a special gift for Grandfather," Ana told her brother Felipe.

"Why don't we make some drawings?" asked Felipe.

Ana knew Grandfather would like drawings. Grandfather always put their drawings on the wall.

"No," Ana said. "Every time we visit Grandfather, we bring drawings. I want to do something special."

It was time to go to Grandfather's. Everyone's gifts for Grandfather were wrapped. Some were wrapped in drawings. Ana helped her father put the gifts in the car. She knew Grandfather would be happy. Still, Ana thought it would be better if they had something special.

On the way, Ana and Felipe tried to think of something special for Grandfather. They couldn't think of anything.

Ana found some slips of paper in the back seat. She picked them up.

"Read what the slip says," Felipe said. Ana read, "Jan's Car Wash. We will wash your car for free."

Ana asked, "Mom? Dad? What are these slips?"

Father looked at the slips. "Some places give out these slips. You can trade the slips in. You can trade that slip for a car wash."

They drove into the yard. Grandfather came out to greet everyone.

"¡*Abuelo*!" Felipe and Ana shouted as they ran to their grandfather.

"*Mi hijo, mi hija*," said Grandfather.

Felipe liked being called *mi hijo*. It's a special way of saying "my son." The words made Felipe feel good inside.

Felipe liked his grandfather's house. There was a big tree in the front yard. There was a garden in the back yard. Good things grew in the garden.

Inside the house, everyone sat down to eat lunch. All through lunch, Grandfather told some jokes. Everyone laughed. Ana thought Grandfather told the best jokes. She still wished she could think of something special to give him.

"I hope you like everything, *Abuelo*," Ana said as Grandfather opened his gifts.

Grandfather smiled and said, "Every time I see you and Felipe, it's like getting a gift."

Then Ana knew what to give Grandfather.

In the next room, Ana told Felipe her plan. "We'll surprise *Abuelo* again," Ana said.

Felipe and Ana worked for a long time. They wrote and wrote.

Everything was ready. The special gift was in a box and wrapped up. Felipe and Ana gave the gift to Grandfather and said, " Surprise, *Abuelo!*"

" I've never had so many surprises, " Grandfather said. He opened the gift. There were slips of paper in the box.

Grandfather read a slip. It said, "We will weed the garden for you."

He read another slip. It said, "We will rake the leaves under the tree."

Grandfather looked at another slip. "This one is good for one song," he said.

Father picked up a slip. "*Abuelo* will like this slip," he said. "It's good for three jokes."

Everyone laughed.

"You can use a slip when we come to visit," Ana told Grandfather. "You can trade a slip for something you would like us to do."

Grandfather hugged Felipe and Ana and said, "Your gift is very special. This visit is the best one ever."

CHECKPOINT

Write each sentence using the correct word.

1. My father _____ to open the car door, but it was stuck.

  smiled   tried   having

2. Her aunt _____ birthday parties were fun.

  visits   wrapped   decided

3. I need a _____ on how to use the telephone.

  lesson   garden   balloon

4. The _____ desk rocked from side to side.

  sadly   wobbly   worry

Write the sentence that best tells what the story is about.

5. Jenny stood up. She took the plates and glasses into the kitchen. She put everything into the sink. Then she turned on the water and filled the sink. It was Jenny's turn to wash the dishes.

  a. Jenny went to the kitchen.

  b. Jenny put everything into the sink.

  c. It was Jenny's turn to wash the dishes.

6. Nicky was late for his aunt's birthday party. He ran upstairs to get the gift for his aunt. He rushed down again and pulled open the door. He ran to the car where his mother was waiting. "I'm ready now," he said.

    a. Nicky ran upstairs to get the gift.

    b. Nicky was late for the birthday party.

    c. Nicky ran to the car.

Read the sentences. Write *yes* on your paper if it could happen. Write *no* on your paper if it could not happen.

7. Nicky uses a fiddle to eat his dinner.

8. Elizabeth hurt her wrist playing baseball.

9. Ben paddled faster than everyone and won the boat race.

10. The bird took a ton of bricks to make her nest.

Decoding: Vowel *o*, Consonant *wr*, doubled consonant before *-le*, drop *e* before *-ed*

41

MEET JACK KENT

When I was very small, I drew pictures.
All children do.
But most children grow out of it.
I never did.
When I learned to write, I put words
with my drawings.
They were funny words and funny drawings.
Such funny drawings are called cartoons.
So I was called a cartoonist.
Now I write books for children.
I still write funny words and
draw funny pictures.
But I'm not a cartoonist now.

Now I'm an author.

My funny words and pictures are in books.

That's how you can tell I'm an author.

It's fun to write a story.

Getting the idea is the hard thing.

But everything I ever did

or saw

or heard

or felt

has an idea in it.

So all I have to do is look about

inside my head.

In time, I find an idea to share with you.

43

An Old Kitten Is a Cat
Jack Kent

Jenny went to the telephone to call her friend Sally. She telephoned to tell Sally about her new pet.

"Guess what!" said Jenny. "I have a new kitten!"

Sally giggled. "ALL kittens are new, Jenny! An OLD kitten is a CAT!"

"Well, anyway," said Jenny, "this kitten is new to me. It's just a furry little ball. I love to hear the kitten purr when I rub it."

Sally said she was glad Jenny had a kitten.

Sally was talking to Tom on the telephone. She told Tom about Jenny's new pet. "Jenny likes to rub her kitten to make it purr," Sally said.

"Rubber kitten, did you say?" asked Tom.

"Yes," said Sally. "She likes to rub her kitten."

"How strange!" said Tom.

Tom telephoned Lin to tell her about Jenny's kitten. "Jenny has a rubber kitten that purrs," said Tom.

"That could be, I guess," said Lin. "I have a rubber mouse that squeaks."

"What next!" said Tom.

When Mel called, Lin told him about Jenny's kitten.

"Jenny has a rubber kitten, and it purrs," she said.

"Did you say Jenny has a rubber mitten in her purse?" asked Mel.

"Yes, Jenny has a rubber kitten, and it purrs," said Lin. "Did you ever hear of such a thing?"

"I never did," said Mel. He giggled at the thought.

After he hung up the telephone, Mel thought about what Lin had told him. "Why would Jenny carry a rubber mitten in her purse?" he wondered.

Mel's telephone rang. It was his friend Tony. Tony had called to chat. Mel asked Tony if he knew that Jenny had a mitten in her purse. "It's rubber," Mel said.

"Robber, did you say?" asked Tony.

"Yes, I said rubber," said Mel. "It was in her purse."

"Oh, no," said Tony. "This is the first I heard about Jenny's purse."

After Mel hung up, Tony called Carmen. "A robber stole Jenny's purse!" said Tony.

"That's too bad!" said Carmen. "What did she carry in the purse?"

"I can't remember what Mel told me," said Tony. "Let me try to remember. Was it some knitting? No. Was it something written? No. Oh! I remember! It was a KITTEN! Yes! Jenny had a kitten in her purse."

"Why would Jenny carry a kitten in her purse?" Carmen wondered.

"I don't know," said Tony. "Maybe the kitten was too small to walk."

"How sad that a robber stole the kitten!" said Carmen.

48

Carmen telephoned Jenny to tell her how sorry she was. "I just heard about your kitten," Carmen said.

"You should see it!" said Jenny. "It's the best little kitten ever!"

"But I thought . . . ," Carmen began. She didn't know what to say. "If a robber stole Jenny's kitten, how could she have a kitten now?" Carmen wondered. Then she thought she had the answer.

"Oh!" said Carmen. "You got a NEW kitten."

Jenny giggled. "ALL kittens are new, Carmen. An OLD kitten is a CAT!"

LIFE SKILL: Telephone Hints

In the last story, the children were not sure what their friends said. Does that ever happen to you? If it does, here are some telephone hints. They might help you.

When you talk on the telephone, speak clearly. It is sometimes hard to hear over the telephone. If you speak clearly, you will be heard better.

When you answer the telephone, greet the caller. Say "Hello."

It is good to ask some questions on the telephone. A question you might ask is "Who's calling?" Can you think of any other things to ask?

Rick Please call
Carlos at 555-3692
Maria

Sometimes, the call is for someone who is not home. Ask the caller to leave a message. Write down the caller's name and telephone number. Leave the message where it will be seen. Some families have a special place to leave messages. Does yours?

Now pretend you are talking on the telephone. Get a partner. First, pretend that one of you is calling the other. Then pretend that the call is for someone who is not there.

Remember: Speak clearly.

Greet the caller.

Ask questions.

Take a message.

Leave the message in a special place.

They Work So You Can Talk

Patricia Ann Lynch

Can you guess what it would be like to have no telephones? You would have to visit everyone you wanted to talk to!

Many people work so that you can make a telephone call. Each telephone company worker has a special job. Would you like to meet some people who work so that you can talk?

The worker most of you know is the operator. When you dial 0, the operator answers. Operators help people when something is wrong. They help people who cannot dial a number. If you cannot reach a number, the operator will help.

It is better to dial your own calls. Then the operator can help those who really need help.

The installer is another telephone worker. The installer may put new telephones in homes and offices.

When a telephone does not work, sometimes an installer is called. The installer will fix the telephone when something is wrong. The installer fixes lines, too. This installer climbed up to find out what went wrong.

Your telephone is joined to the telephone company by a wire. Workers make sure the wire is joined to the right place. That way, you have your own telephone number. Your friend has his or her own number, too.

Special equipment joins your telephone to your friend's. Then you can talk. Special workers take care of this equipment. They must have a lot of training.

Sometimes, rain or wind hurts outside telephone wires. Sometimes, wires that go under the ground are cut. When wires are not working, workers have to find out what is wrong. They have special tools to help them.

These workers help people get new telephones. They answer questions people may have. They will see that someone comes to fix your telephone.

Telephone companies are always looking for good workers. They have people who try to find new workers. These people visit schools. They tell about the jobs the telephone company has.

Would you like to join the telephone company team ? Which job would you like best?

I HAVE A SISTER

I have a sister
who likes to go with me
out to the grassy lot
behind our house.
Today we are stalking deer.

I turn to speak to her.
I use no voice,
just my fingers and my lips.
She understands,
and walks behind me,
stepping where I step.

I am the one who listens
for small sounds.
She is the one who watches
for quick movements in the grass.

I have a sister.
My sister is deaf.

Jeanne Whitehouse Peterson

Frederick's Alligator

Esther Allen Peterson

One morning, Frederick said to his mom, "I have a pet lion in my room. We are pals."

"Sure, Frederick," said his mom. "Now eat your eggs. You will be late for school."

At school, Frederick said, "I have a bear at home."

"Sure, Frederick," said his teacher. "Now please take your seat."

On the way home from school, Frederick went to the river. He went to look for wild animals. All he found was an egg in the mud and an old shoe box.

Frederick put the egg in the shoe box. Then he packed the box with mud and leaves. He carried it home and hid it under his bed.

Frederick looked at the egg every day. One morning, it moved. Then it began to crack. At last, it hatched.

Out came a baby alligator.

"Yonk, yonk," it said.

Frederick put the alligator on the floor. It yawned. Then it tried out its wobbly legs.

Frederick put the alligator in a pan of water. He hid it under his bed and went to his mom.

"I have a baby alligator under my bed," said Frederick.

"That's nice," said his mom. "I hope your lion doesn't eat it."

The next day at school, he said, "I have a baby alligator under my bed. May I bring it to school?"

"Sure, Frederick," said his teacher. "You may bring your bear, too."

The next morning, Frederick put his alligator in the shoe box. He carried it to the kitchen.

"Frederick!" said his mom. "You do have an alligator!"

"I sure do," he said. "My teacher said I can bring it to school."

When he got to school, everyone said, "Frederick! You do have an alligator!"

Frederick said, "I found an egg near the river. I carried it home and put it under my bed. In a little while, the egg hatched. The alligator eats bugs, worms, and cat food."

The teacher said, "Frederick, please put your alligator in the back with the tadpoles and worms."

At noon, the alligator was missing. The tadpoles and the worms were missing, too.

The children looked under their seats. They looked in the bookcase. Frederick's alligator could not be found. Frederick was upset all day.

At the end of the day, a friend was putting on his boots. "Here it is!" he shouted.

Frederick put his alligator in the box and carried it home. "I don't think I should keep you," he said. "When you get big, you might eat my tadpole."

Frederick thought and thought. Then he carried the alligator back to the river.

"Good-by," he said. "I thought you would be a nice pet. But I guess I'll stick to tadpoles and maybe white mice."

At home, his mom didn't think there was a lion in his room, but she looked anyway. His friends still wonder if he has a bear at home. But Frederick won't tell.

CHECKPOINT

Write each sentence using the correct word.

1. I can't _____ where I put the baby alligator.

   carry   wondered   remember

2. _____ live under the ground.

   Worms   Pictures   Mitten

3. Many workers work at our _____.

   lions   company   children

4. I could hear the kitten _____.

   purr   purse   river

Write the sentence that best tells what the story is about.

5. Gail decided to visit her grandfather's farm. When she got there, she saw baby ducks splashing in the pond. Near the farmhouse, chickens were pecking at their feed. Cows were off on a hill. Gail's grandfather was working in the garden.

   a. Gail saw ducks at her grandfather's farm.

   b. Gail visited her grandfather's farm.

   c. Gail's grandfather had a garden.

6. The clouds were growing dark. Big drops of rain started falling. A cold wind blew across the flat land. Tom pulled on his mittens. He walked on, wrapping his coat around him. It wasn't a good night to be outside.

    a. Big drops of rain started to fall.

    b. The land was flat.

    c. It wasn't a good night outside.

Write *S* if the words have almost the same meaning. Write *O* if the words have almost opposite meanings.

Decoding: Drop *e* before *-ing;* change *y* to *i* before *-ed, -es, -er*

  7. filled—emptied

  8. messier—neater

  9. stories—tales

10. still—moving

11. wishing—hoping

12. giving—taking

Look

Our planet's name is Earth. It is a beautiful place. If you look up high, you might spot a cloud moving across the sky. If you look down low, you might spot a fish swimming in the water.

Now let's look around this unit. What does the Earth give to us? There's water to drink or swim in. In the water, you'll look at Andre, a very special seal. In the sky, you might not see the wind, but you will hear it. The wind has something to tell you.

You can start looking right now "by the sandy water . . . ."

High and Low

67

By the sandy water I breathe in the odor of
the sea;
From there the wind comes and blows over
the world.
By the sandy water I breathe in the odor
of the sea;
From there the clouds come and rain falls
over the world.

Papago song

68

Fish Story

Robert Tallon

"I've got to get out of here!" Little Fish said. "I'm tired of swimming in the same water. I want a bigger pond."

Big Cat, walking by, heard him. "May I be of help?" Big Cat asked.

"I want to see the world," Little Fish said.

"The world is beautiful up here, really beautiful," Big Cat said. "The flowers and the trees are beautiful. So is the ocean just over the hill."

" Ocean ! Old Fish told me about the ocean," Little Fish said. "Can you take me there?"

"Sure," said Big Cat. "First, I'll have to go home and get a bag to carry you in."

"Please hurry back," Little Fish said.

Big Cat came back with a big bag. He put it into the water. Little Fish swam inside.

"Thank you," Little Fish said.

"I'm glad to help a friend," Big Cat said. He licked his lips.

Big Cat ran through the woods.

"How beautiful! Is that a flower?" Little Fish asked.

"It's a flower," Big Cat growled.

"Could we stop?" Little Fish asked.

"No," Big Cat yelled.

"Where is the ocean?" Little Fish asked.

"Just over the hill," Big Cat said. "Now, quiet! You're asking too many questions."

"I'm sorry," Little Fish said. "It's so new to me."

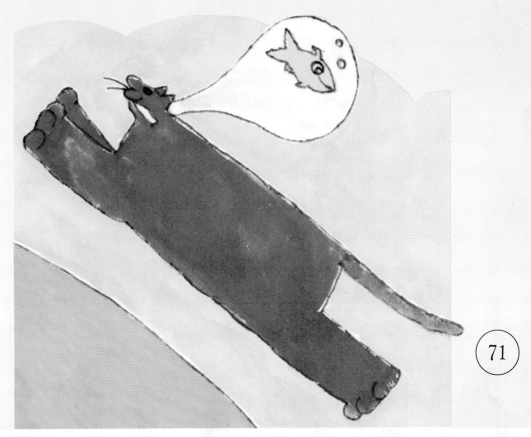

Big Cat ran over the hill and into a house. Little Fish looked around at the pots and pans on the walls. "Is this the ocean?" he asked.

"No. It's my kitchen," Big Cat said. "I'm going to cook you!"

Little Fish shook. "Why me?" he asked.

Big Cat sang to himself as he got a pan ready. "Didn't Old Fish ever tell you about Cats and Fishes?" he asked.

"Are you a Cat?" Little Fish asked.

"Yes, Big Cat's the name. And I'm going to eat you."

"But I'm all bones," Little Fish cried.

"Quiet! I'm trying to read this cookbook," Big Cat said. "I'm starved!"

"Big Cat, wait, please!" Little Fish yelled. "Just look at me. I'm all bones. I'd be just a snack for you. But I know a Big Fish. He's so big, he'd fill this kitchen."

Big Cat looked at Little Fish. "Just where is this big fish?" he asked.

"Back at the pond. He's big enough to last you a month," Little Fish said. "If you take me back, I'll get him for you."

"How?" Big Cat asked.

"Have you got some ketchup?" Little Fish asked.

"What if I do?" Big Cat answered.

"He just loves ketchup. Just take me back," Little Fish said. " Bring a string and some ketchup. Leave the rest to me."

Big Cat took up the bag with Little Fish. He took another bag with the ketchup and raced back to the pond. He put Little Fish into the pond. Then he let down the string with the ketchup.

Little Fish swam out of the bag. "How wonderful to be back in my beautiful pond," he thought. He swam around and around.

Big Cat jiggled the string. "Hurry up, Little Fish. Get your friend. I'm starved!" he said.

Little Fish grabbed the string and swam down with it. "OK, Big Cat," Little Fish called. "Pull it up!"

Big Cat pulled on the string. He pulled and pulled—and landed his catch. It was an old bike!

" You tricked me ! " Big Cat yelled. He jumped up and down.

Little Fish laughed as he swam to the center of the pond. "It was just a Fish Story," he sang out. "It was just a Fish Story for a Big Cat!"

Andre:
A Very Special Seal

Suzanne Higgins

In Rockport, Maine, I saw a big, gray statue. I have seen many statues. Most are of important people. This statue was a surprise. It was a statue of a seal! What could a seal have done that was so important?

I wanted to know. So I asked a woman about the statue.

"That statue?" she said. "Oh, that's our Andre. He's a very important seal!"

This is what I found out about Andre.

A man named Goodridge found Andre in the ocean. Andre was about three days old. There was no mother seal in sight. Mr. Goodridge thought the little seal would starve. So he took it home with him.

The Goodridge family loved animals. They had many pets. Mr. Goodridge felt that one more pet would be just fine! So the baby seal joined the family. He was named Andre.

Raising a baby seal was not an easy job. Andre didn't know how to feed himself. If Andre didn't eat, he would not live. Mr. Goodridge had to think of a way to get Andre to eat.

He made a special baby bottle for Andre. He made a hole in a log. Then he covered the log with rubber. Andre's bottle fit into the hole in the log. Andre liked this special bottle. He grew bigger and stronger every day.

Mr. Goodridge found an old bathtub. He filled it with water. This was Andre's bed at night.

In the day, Andre played in the house or in the yard. Sometimes, he chased the family dog out of its house. When he was sleepy, he could nap in the dog's house!

When Andre was older, he needed fish to eat. Each day, Mr. Goodridge put Andre in the back of his car. He took Andre to the ocean for a swim. Soon the baby seal began to catch his own food.

Andre had learned to fish quickly. Mr. Goodridge knew he could learn other things as well.

Mr. Goodridge found it easy to teach Andre all kinds of tricks. Andre loved to show off! He would do tricks any time people were around. Andre loved to make people happy. Soon, he had made many friends.

In the summer, there were always people around. But the winters in Maine are cold. Not many people are around in the winter. Andre would get very lonely. Sometimes Andre went looking for friends. He would swim to a boat. Andre was big and strong now. Even just playing, he could tip a small boat over.

Mr. Goodridge was afraid that Andre might hurt someone. Even more, he was afraid that someone might hurt Andre! He knew he had to find a winter home for Andre.

Mr. Goodridge knew about a special place in Boston, Massachusetts. It was the New England Aquarium. An aquarium is a zoo for fish and other sea animals. At some aquariums, sea animals do tricks. Lots of people visit these aquariums. They come to look at the fish. They come to see the water shows.

Mr. Goodridge wanted the aquarium to take Andre for the winter. He knew Andre would be happy there. Andre could show off his many tricks. Best of all, he would not be lonely.

The New England Aquarium was happy to take Andre. Now Andre could live in the aquarium every winter.

Andre liked the aquarium. Mr. Goodridge visited him a lot. Andre was always happy to see Mr. Goodridge.

Each summer, Andre was set free in the ocean. Each summer, Andre found his own way back to Rockport, Maine. He swam by himself the whole way.

People along the way looked for Andre. They called Mr. Goodridge to tell him they had seen Andre. Mr. Goodridge was happy that people cared so much about Andre.

Even the newspapers told about Andre. Each day, they told where Andre had been seen. After all, Andre was a very special seal! Summers in Rockport, Maine, would not be the same without him.

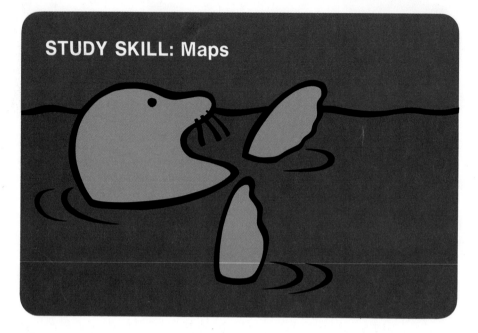

STUDY SKILL: Maps

Each year Andre swam from Boston, Massachusetts, to Rockport, Maine. It was a long trip. Sometimes when you take a trip, you use a map to help you find your way.

On the next page is a map of the coast from Massachusetts to Maine. The dark line shows Andre's route between Boston and Rockport.

There are two symbols on the map. The first symbol is called a *compass rose.* This tells you which way north, south, east, and west are. On most maps, north is at the top.

The second symbol tells you the *scale* of the map. A map cannot show the real size of a place. Places on a map are made much smaller. Here the scale tells you that one inch (2.54 cm) on the map stands for 80 miles (128.7 km) in real life.

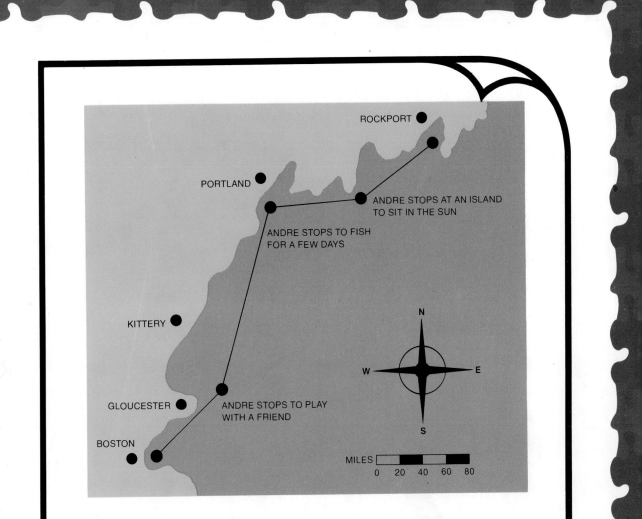

Look at the map. Which symbol on the map will help you answer these questions?

1. Andre left Boston to swim to Rockport. Did he swim north or south?

2. How far did Andre swim before he stopped to play with his friends?

3. When Andre stopped at the island, how many miles were left to Rockport?

Anansi Finds a Fool

African Folktale retold by Verna Aardema

Anansi lived long ago. He was not like the others in his village. Anansi was greedy and lazy. He was always up to some trick. One day Anansi went looking for a fool to go fishing. He wanted someone to do the work while he got the fish!

His friend Anene knew of his plans. Anene thought of a way to teach Anansi a lesson. He said, "Anansi, I'll go fishing with you. Two can catch fish better than one."

"Fine!" cried Anansi. "We'll be partners."

First they had to make a fish trap. So they found some big trees. Anene said, "Anansi, I'll cut the branches. You can get tired for me."

"Wait," said Anansi. "Why should I get tired for you?"

"When there's work to do, someone has to get tired," said Anene. "If I do the work, you should get tired for me!"

Anansi said, "I'll cut the branches. You get tired!"

Up the tree went Anansi. *Kra, kra, kra* went his knife as he cut off the branches.

While Anansi worked, Anene sat under the tree. He pretended to get tired. He moaned, "*Wolu, wolu, wolu.*"

Soon the branches were cut. Anene said, "I'll make the fish trap. It's my turn to work. It's your turn to get tired."

"Wait," said Anansi. "You are doing well at getting tired. Keep on getting tired. I'll make the fish trap myself."

Anansi worked. Anene pretended to get very tired. He pretended so well that he fell onto his back.

Soon the trap was ready. Anene said, "It's my turn to work now. I'll set the trap. There are crocodiles in the lake. If one bites me, you can die for me."

"No!" cried Anansi. "Do you think I am a fool? I'll set the trap. If a crocodile bites me, you can die for me!" So Anansi took the trap into the water.

The next morning there were three fish in the trap. Anene said, "You take these fish, Anansi. I'll take my turn next time."

"Wait!" cried Anansi. "The trap is just starting to work. You take these fish. I'll take my turn next."

So Anene took the three fish to market and sold them.

The next day, there were six fish in the trap. "Look!" cried Anene. "Every day gets better! It's your turn today, Anansi!"

"Oh, no!" said Anansi. "You want to wait for a bigger catch! Well, you take these. I'll take my turn next time!"

So Anene took the six fish to market and sold them.

The next day there were twelve fish in the trap. "Anansi!" cried Anene. "There are twelve fish today! Too bad they are such little ones."

Anansi looked at the fish. "It's my turn," he said. "But these fish are too small. You take them. I'll take my turn next time!"

So Anene took the twelve little fish to market and sold them.

The next day there were no fish at all in the trap! The trap had spoiled in the water. Fish might have come into it. But they would have gone *bu-tu-ru* out through the holes.

Anene said, "Anansi, too bad the trap is spoiled. I think I'll take the trap to the market and sell it."

"Wait!" cried Anansi. "You got all the fish! Now you want the trap, too! I'll sell it myself!"

92

Anansi put the spoiled fish trap on his head. He went to the market. He sang, "Fish trap for sale! Fish trap for sale!"

The head man saw Anansi. He said, "What is this! You're trying to sell a spoiled fish trap! You will be punished."

So Anansi was punished. He had to wear the trap on his head all day. Everyone laughed.

Anansi turned to Anene. He said, "What kind of partner are you? I am the one being punished. You should be the one being laughed at!"

Anene said, "Anansi, you wanted a fool to go fishing with you. You didn't have to look far! You were the fool!"

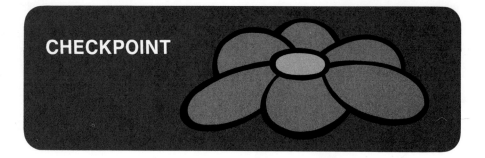

CHECKPOINT

Write each sentence using the correct word.

rest   punished   branches

pretended   statue   even

1. Mom _____ the dog when it dug up the flowers.

2. Lou stood as still as a _____.

3. Grace _____ to be asleep when her mother looked in.

4. Seals are so smart, they can _____ do tricks.

Write the best answer to each question.

Beth's family went to an open-air market. The sun was shining, and a cool wind blew off the ocean. It was a beautiful summer day. Beth's father wanted to look at the flowers for sale. Beth's mother wanted to look at the books for sale. They decided to look at both the flowers and the books.

5. Where did Beth's family go?

    a. to the aquarium

    b. to an open-air market

    c. to a play

6. Who wanted to look at the flowers for sale?

    a. Beth

    b. Beth's mother

    c. Beth's father

Write each sentence using the correct word.

Decoding:
Vowel *ie*;
Suffixes *-ly*, *-y*

7. I talked _____ with my mother last night.

    hilly   bossy   briefly

8. The field was soft, _____; and green.

    hungry   grassy   ground

9. We waited _____ as they slowly passed.

    pushy   patiently   only

THE WIND

Who has seen the wind?
　　Neither I nor you;
But when the leaves hang trembling
　　The wind is passing through.

Who has seen the wind?
　　Neither you nor I;
But when the trees bow down their heads
　　The wind is passing by.

Christina Rossetti

Wind Is to Feel

Shirley Cook Hatch

What is wind? Wind is air that is moving.

Reach out your hand. What do you feel? Your hand is in the air. But it feels nothing touch it.

Stand by an open window when the curtains are moving. You feel the wind blow in the window. The wind blows the curtains. It blows on you. You can catch the curtains and hold them still. You cannot catch the wind. You feel the wind. But you do not see the wind. You cannot touch the wind.

Blow on your fingers. Do you feel the air touch your fingers? Wet your hands. Now blow on them. Do you feel the air? When air moves over your wet hands, your fingers feel cool.

When you go swimming on a hot day, you feel cool, too. Air moves over your wet skin and cools you.

Wind feels different when it blows over water and land. Wind coming over water is damp. Wind that blows over land feels dry. If wind blows over warm water or land, it will feel warm. If wind blows over cool water or land, it will feel cool.

You can feel warm air moving when you blow on something hot. The moving air takes some of the heat with it.

Wind makes many things move. Little trees can bend with the wind. Sometimes pieces of big, old trees snap off.

Wind blows plant seeds through the air. Many of these seeds grow in new places. Wind brings the rain that helps plants grow.

Did you ever see a weather vane? Wind pushes a weather vane. The weather vane shows where the wind comes from. You can see things move with the wind. But you cannot see the wind.

Wind makes sounds. Blow across the top of a bottle. What do you hear?

Blow up a balloon. Let the air out slowly. Do you hear a funny noise? Blow the balloon up again. Let it go. Does it make a different noise?

Wind can make music. Can you whistle? Whistle a tune. You have made music with wind. Some musical instruments are called wind instruments. We blow into them to make music.

The next time you see a band, look at the people. Do they puff out their cheeks as they play? They are making music with wind.

Wind can tell you of things that are near you. It brings different smells as it passes by you. From smells, you can sometimes tell where the wind has come from.

Wind may bring the smell of new bread. Wind may bring the smell of cows from a farm. It may bring the smell of newly cut grass.

Wind brings your nose signals that you cannot hear or see or feel.

Wind can help us work, too. Windmills can bring water from wells deep in the ground. Then people can water their gardens when there is no rain.

Wind makes sailboats go. The sail catches the wind. It pulls the boat through the water. If the wind stops, the boat will stop.

Sometimes wind is too strong for small boats. Then the small boats must stay tied up.

Now you know that wind is made when air is moving. Wind makes things move. You can see the things move. Wind makes sounds. You can hear the sounds. Wind can come from different places. Sometimes the wind brings smells.

The wind does all these things. Still, you cannot see the wind. Sometimes the wind is cool. Sometimes the wind is warm.

The wind is to feel.

SCIENCE READING: What's It All About?

Wind helps us. It can make sailboats go. It can dry wet clothes. It can blow the clouds away.

Wind is moving air. Why does air move? Where does wind come from? You can find answers to such questions as these in science books.

TAKE A FIRST LOOK

Look at the next page. It tells about an activity. You can find out things by doing an activity. Look at the girl doing the activity. What is she doing? What do you think she is going to find out?

FIND THE KEY IDEAS

The activity has three parts. What are the names of the three parts? Which part tells *what* the activity is going to show? Which part tells *how* the activity is done? Which part tells *why* something happens?

READ CAREFULLY

Now read about the activity. What does heat do to air? The same thing can happen to the air on earth. How does this activity help show one way wind is made? Can you guess what heats the air on earth?

EXPANDING AIR

What: To see air expand when it is heated. *Expand* means "take up more space."

How: Put a balloon over the top of an empty bottle. The bottle is not really empty. It has air inside. Put the bottle with the balloon in a pan. Fill the pan with hot water. Wait a minute or so. The balloon will expand because the air expands.

Why: The hot water heats the air in the bottle. The air expands. It needs more space than there is inside the bottle. So some of the expanded air leaves the bottle. It goes inside the balloon. The heated air blows up the balloon.

105

What the Wind Told

Betty Boegehold

Tossy was tired of being sick. She was tired of staying in bed. She was tired of looking out her window at all the other windows across the way. She was tired of listening to the wind.

"Stop blowing, Wind," she said. "Tell me a story."

"All right," said the Wind. "What shall I tell you?"

Tossy thought. Then she said, "Tell me about the windows across the way."

"Very well," said the Wind. "After all, windows are named after me. Pick your window. Then I will tell you a story."

Tossy looked at the windows. "Tell me about that woman," she said. "Why does she lean out her window every day?"

The Wind said, "The woman has to lean out her window every day. Every day, at ten o'clock, her floor turns into a pond! If she didn't lean out her window, she would get wet.

"The woman has some furniture, of course," the Wind said. "It is all nailed high up on the walls. The chairs, the table, the stove, and the bed are on the walls. When the floor switches to water, the furniture stays dry."

The Wind said, "The woman has a cat, too. He sits on the table. He stares into the water, looking for fish to catch."

"Does he ever get one?" asked Tossy.

"No," said the Wind. "He never has time. Every day, at twelve o'clock, the floor comes back again. The cat jumps down from the table. He walks around. But not the woman. She keeps looking out the window."

"Does the woman like having a pond in her room every day?" asked Tossy.

"Oh, yes," said the Wind. "That way, she never has to wash her floor."

The second day, Tossy said to the Wind, "Tell me about the window with five plants in it. Who lives in that window?"

"The Plants live there," said the Wind. "Only the Plants. Mr. and Mrs. Plant, Grandma Plant, Aunt Cactus, and Uncle Bean live there.

"The five little plants in the window are their children. The Plants put the children out in the spring. They take them inside in the winter."

The Wind said, "Of course, there is only deep dirt on the floor. There are lots of worms in it. A little puddle is in the middle. There are holes in the roof, so the rain comes in. Nobody there cares about a muddy floor.

"They haven't a TV, of course. They listen to garden talks on the radio. Mr. and Mrs. Plant, Grandma Plant, Aunt Cactus, and Uncle Bean like a quiet life."

"I'm sorry for the Plant children outside the window all summer," said Tossy.

"Don't be," said the Wind. "They don't mind. They can stay up as late as they like."

On the last day, Tossy was well. The sun was shining. The sky was blue. No wind was blowing outside her window.

"Oh, well," Tossy thought. "The wind will always blow back again. It will tell me more stories when I want to hear them."

IN THE WIND

Doris Van Liew Foster

Weather signs told of a storm. The sun had turned away. The sky was muddy yellow. It was a strange sky color. The palm trees stood tall and quiet. It was the quiet that was the most strange.

Before long, wind and rain broke the quiet.

Small animals looked for places to hide. A squirrel ran to a hole in a tree.

The storm came slowly. It became bigger and bigger. Its sides went out a long way. Sometimes it stood resting, catching its breath.

The storm grew. It was no longer just a storm. It was a hurricane.

The radio told how strong the hurricane's winds were. It told what its course was. The radio said, "The storm is headed this way. It has picked up speed over the water. If it doesn't change course, it will hit today. Keep listening for weather news."

Stephen helped his father put storm shutters on the windows. They brought small things inside.

"What is a hurricane?" Stephen asked.

His father thought about it. "A hurricane is a big cone of spinning air. The winds in the wall of a hurricane go very fast. All the warm, damp air goes to the center of the storm. The closer to the center it gets, the faster it spins. But the very center of the storm is quiet. We call this quiet the eye of the storm."

All this while, the storm was coming closer. Now rain began to beat at the houses. The heads of palm trees bent down. Their leaves turned faster and faster until they looked like rags. Slowly the rain hid the sky until it could not be seen.

A hurricane has a sound, a beat, like no other wind. That sound was starting now— BOOM, SWISH—BOOM, SWISH.

A hurricane sometimes brings gifts. This one did.

From the sea, the storm dug shells of different colors and shapes. It spread them on the beach.

From the air, the hurricane took something so small that it slid from its hold. It fell to the ground near Stephen's house. Stephen saw that it was a bird and ran outside to get it.

The bird was quiet in Stephen's hand. He held it close to him. He ran back inside.

Stephen showed the bird to his father. "I wish it would open its eyes," he said.

"Maybe you were in time to save the bird," his father said. "It needs to be kept warm and dry."

Stephen looked in his room for something to put the bird in. He thought, "If I got lost in a storm, I'd want someone to find me and keep me warm."

At last he found a box the right size. His old coat would make a soft bed. "Little bird, this shoe box will be your bed." He put the bird inside.

117

All day the storm blew. Far into the night, it kept the moon and stars out of sight.

Small animals stayed out of sight. Stephen covered the bird for the night.

In the morning, the radio said, "The storm is no longer a danger. It has moved out to sea. In the night, its winds slowed. It cannot be called a hurricane now."

Once again the sun was shining in a blue sky. A squirrel played in a tree. Birds flew in happy company.

People came out into the sun. They wanted to see what the storm had done. They found streets blocked by trees. Telephone lines were down.

Stephen and his father brought the bird outside. Could this bright little bird be that wet rag saved from the storm?

When Stephen put the bird down, it hopped over the ground. It cried out.

Stephen and his father waited. Would the mother bird hear her baby?

The answer soon came. A big jay flew down. She called to her baby.

119

The young jay was in its mother's care. Stephen's father said, "Let's walk along the beach."

The waves were high. The gulls were calling and turning in the sky. Stephen picked up shells. He kept flinging them away until he found one he liked.

"Look at this shell," he cried. "It looks like the wing of a bird." He turned the shell slowly in his hands. He ran his finger along the lines of color.

"I am going to keep this always," he said.

CHECKPOINT

Write the word that does not belong with the others.

1. chairs   table   curtains   until

2. storm   weather   stories   hurricane

3. warm   statue   cool   hot

4. fingers   speed   rush   hurry

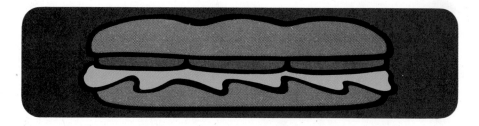

Write each sentence using the correct word.

5. I _____ two books yesterday.

   read   reed   red

6. The wind _____ my hat off.

   bloom   blue   blew

7. Please sit over _____.

   their   there   they're

8. I _____ my lunch as quickly as I could.

   eight   a   ate

Write the best answer to the question.

Stephen and Gail decided to paint a picture for their mother. They found some paper and paint in Stephen's room. They worked all morning. They left the picture to dry while they ate lunch. Of course, when they came back, they weren't sure if they should touch it.

9. What did Stephen and Gail find in Stephen's room?

    a. They found their mother.

    b. They found their lunch.

    c. They found paper and paint.

Write each sentence using the correct word.

10. We slowly climbed the _____ path.

    chilly   hilly   hitting

11. They _____ put the boxes next to the wall.

    highly   neatly   night

12. The puffy clouds moved _____.

    quickly   quiet   dimly

Come here—just a little closer. Bring your listening ears with you. Come and hear some tales. These tales tell you things. They tell *why, what, where,* and *who.*

Listen to a fine feather of a tale. It tells *why* a crow is as proud as a peacock. Then tickle yourself with a bird of another feather. Hear a tale about talking turkeys. *What* did the turkeys tell? After that, you'll get into a pickle about pickles. But *where* are the pickles? Sniff Billy's lunch box for the answer. By the way, what do both people and corn have? They both have ears!

What about *who*? *Who* tells the tales? The *who* is *you*! Turn the page and read about *you*.

ckle

Tales

nd Corn

Ears

Where Tales Come From

Once upon a time, long, long ago, families had no TV to look at. Children had no schools to go to. People had no books to read. Yet there were always stories to hear.

People told stories to their children. When the children grew up, they told stories to *their* children. And so it went.

Now these old stories and tales have been written down. Boys and girls of today can read them and hear them, too.

Some of the tales tell why things came to be. People who lived long ago looked around them. They asked questions about what they saw.

Some of the questions they asked are these: Why is the sea salty? How did the fox get a white tip on its tail?

People made up stories to answer these questions.

Some of the tales we read are about kings and queens. Some stories are about animals who talk and act like people. Other stories are about everyday people. Many of these tales teach a lesson.

Long, long ago, people sat around a fire as night fell. Their work was done, and they rested. A storyteller began a tale. Everyone listened.

People heard about a small animal tricking a big, bad animal. They heard about friends helping or not helping each other. They heard about other people who could be wise or silly. Around the fire, listening to the storytellers, the people heard many tales.

Once upon a time, long, long ago . . .

The Vain Bird and the Peacock Feathers

Aesop Fable, retold

There was once a vain crow. One day the crow walked by a pond. He looked into the pond and saw himself in the water. "Oh, my," he cried. "I had no idea I looked so plain. I knew what other crows looked like. But I didn't know I looked the same."

This made the crow very sad. "More than anything," he said, "I wish I were beautiful."

The vain crow went to his friends to ask them for help. All of his friends just laughed at him. " You are not ugly, " his friends said. " You are a fine-looking crow. You are no different from any other bird."

"My feathers are all the same color. I don't like being plain," answered the vain crow. He looked at the ground and slowly walked away.

"Of course his feathers are all the same color," said one bird when the vain crow had gone. "That's how crows are *supposed* to look!"

The vain crow thought and thought. "How can I make myself beautiful?"

Just then he spied some peacock feathers on the ground. The peacock feathers were beautiful. "What fine feathers! These are just what I need," cried the crow. He quickly stuck the peacock feathers in among his own. "Now I will be as beautiful as a peacock. I will no longer be plain and ugly," he said.

That very afternoon, the vain crow went to visit the other birds again. He wanted to show off his new feathers. The vain crow strutted by his friends.

One bird asked him, "What do you think you are?"

Another bird said, " I guess you think you're better than we are. Well, why don't you find new friends?" The vain crow had hurt his friends' feelings.

131

"Very well," the vain bird said. "I belong with the beautiful birds, anyway. I will go to join the peacocks." He turned and walked away.

Now, it so happened that the crow looked quite foolish with peacock feathers. His friends hadn't told him just how foolish he looked. When the peacocks saw how silly the crow looked, they laughed and laughed. "What a funny sight," they said. Louder and louder they laughed, until tears filled their eyes. Then the peacocks chased the crow away.

When the crow was alone, he thought about how foolish he had been. He was sorry he had been mean. He was sorry he had been treating his friends badly. "I was silly to be vain," he said. Then he plucked out the peacock feathers. He never complained of being plain and ugly again.

The lesson of the story is: *Fine feathers do not make fine birds.*

The Wolf in the Wool Suit

Patricia Ann Lynch

Once there was a wolf who wanted to catch some sheep for dinner. But he had to find a way to trick them.

The wolf saw wool caught on a bush. The wool gave him a great idea! He'd wear a wool suit and look just like a sheep!

The wolf took all the wool he could find. He carded the wool. Next, he spun the wool into yarn. Then he wove the yarn into cloth.

The wolf took the cloth to a tailor. He asked the tailor to make him a suit. The tailor took her shears and cut the cloth. She made the cloth into a fine wool suit.

The wolf tried on his suit. "Now I look just like a sheep!" he thought.

The next day, the wolf sneaked into the flock of sheep. He went up to a lamb. "Why are you eating here?" he asked. "There is a much better patch of grass just over that hill."

"My grandmother told me to stay with other sheep," the lamb said.

"I'll be with you," the wolf said. So the lamb started to go with the wolf.

Just then, the lamb's grandmother saw him with the wolf. "That's a strange sheep," she thought. "He has a wool suit. But he just doesn't look like a sheep." Then she saw the wolf's black nose. "Wolf!" she cried. "See his black nose! Wolf!"

At that, the wolf ran away.

135

The wolf went to a painter. "Will you paint my nose white?" the wolf asked the painter. The painter painted the wolf's nose white.

The next day, the wolf went up to the lamb and asked, "Why are you eating here? There is a fine patch of grass just over that hill. Come with me." So the lamb started to go with the wolf.

Just then, the lamb's grandmother saw him with the wolf. "That's a strange sheep," she thought. "He has a wool suit and a white nose. But he just doesn't look like a sheep." Then she saw the wolf's gray paws. "Wolf!" she cried. "See his gray paws! Wolf!"

At that, the wolf ran away.

"I'll have to dye my paws," the wolf thought. He got some dye. He dyed his paws to match his suit.

The next day, the wolf went up to the lamb and asked, "Why are you eating here? Come with me over that hill where the grass is better." So the lamb started to go with the wolf.

Just then, the lamb's grandmother saw him with the wolf. "That's a strange sheep," she thought. "He has a wool suit. He has a white nose and white feet. But he just doesn't look like a sheep." Then she saw the wolf's sharp teeth. "Wolf!" she cried. "See his sharp teeth! Wolf!"

At that, the wolf ran away.

137

When he got home, the wolf looked at himself. "She's right," he thought. "No sheep has sharp teeth like these." For a while he thought about pulling out his teeth. But how would he eat?

The wolf took off his white suit. He washed the paint off his nose. He washed the dye off his paws. "Some sheep are hard to fool," he thought.

Lesson: You can fool some of the people some of the time. But you can't fool all of the people all of the time.

138

Turkey Girl

Native-American Folktale retold by Beverly V. Hurlbut

My cousin, Jan, has come to visit us. She lives in a very big city. This is her first visit to a Zuñi village. Jan has never lived any place other than a big city. I have never lived any place other than the village. So we live in very different ways.

But we are the same age. So we are alike in some ways.

Yesterday we went on a picnic near a big cave close to our house. By the cave are some big, white rocks. One rock has a hole in it. The hole is like a big window in the rock. The hole is big enough to set a whole house inside.

I like to have picnics by this big rock. I have fun looking through the hole. Jan thought it was fun to look through, too. Then she saw the marks in the white rocks by the cave.

"Oh, look," said Jan. "These funny little marks look like tracks."

My father smiled. "I will tell you a Zuñi story about those tracks," he said.

Long, long ago, the earth was still soft. In the village, there was a girl who took care of the turkeys. From morning to night, she looked after the turkeys. She fed them. She gave them water. She took very good care of them. Because she had to stay with the turkeys, people called her Turkey Girl.

One day Turkey Girl heard of plans for a big dance. She wanted to go. Because she was poor, she didn't have good clothes to wear. She began to cry. The turkeys heard her crying. The biggest turkey said, "Don't cry. We will help you get clothes. You feed us and help us. Now we will help you."

"How can you help me?" asked Turkey Girl.

"Look," said the biggest turkey. He dropped one of his feathers. The feather turned into some lovely clothes.

"Look," said another turkey. She dropped a feather. The feather turned into a lovely ring. The turkeys dropped more feathers. Soon Turkey Girl looked beautiful.

"Go to the dance," said the biggest turkey. "Have fun, but come back soon."

"I will," said the Turkey Girl. Away she ran to the dance.

No one knew her.

"Who is she?" everyone asked. "Who is that beautiful girl?"

Turkey Girl had fun at the dance. She danced and danced. She stayed and stayed. It was getting late.

"The turkeys! Oh, my! I said I would come back soon. Oh, my!" Turkey Girl began to run home. She was too late! The turkeys were gone. Turkey Girl had not come back in time.

"Turkey Girl could hear the turkeys," my father said. " She began to run after them. When she got close to them, they would run. They ran and ran. Turkey Girl ran and ran. She sat down to cry. Still, the turkeys did not stop. They ran far, far away. Turkey Girl never found her turkeys. But they left their tracks behind them. Those are the marks you see here. That was long ago, long ago when the earth was still soft."

"That is a good ending for a story," said Jan. "That was a good story. It makes me think of another story."

Do you know what story Jan was thinking about?

The Pickle Plan

Marilyn Singer

Nobody cares about me. Nobody pays any attention to me.

I think about a lot of things. I wonder why my dog's nose is always cold and mine isn't. I wonder why some flowers smell good and others don't.

I think about why Billy Michaels has pickles every day in his lunch box, but I never do.

But nobody is interested—nobody at all.

Mom says people who are different get lots of attention. So I'm working on a plan. I call it The Different Plan. I tell Mom we're having a spring party in school. I ask her to lend me her hat with the green flower.

She says, "Well, you'll look interesting."

"You mean different?" I ask.

"That's the word," she says.

I wear the hat to school. Billy Michaels pulls out my green flower.

"Give it back," I shout.

Just then, Ms. Ronow, our teacher, comes in. "My, Rachel," she says. "Don't you look different!" I sit up very straight and smile. "But we don't wear hats in class."

I stop smiling.

Dad says people who are mysterious get lots of attention. So I have a new plan. I call this one The Mysterious Plan.

I am trying the plan out on my brother, Larry. I am sitting by the wall. I have a mysterious smile on my face. Once in a while, I laugh—just a little.

"What's so funny?" Larry asks.

I just say, " Nothing. " I use my most mysterious voice.

"Then stop laughing," he says.

" Don't you wonder what I'm thinking about?" I ask him.

"No," he says.

I guess I'll have to think of a third plan.

My cousin says that lively people get lots of attention. So I've decided to try out The Lively Plan.

I'm at my Uncle Ben's. We've just had dinner. "I have a little surprise for everyone," I say.

No one looks very surprised. But I start my act anyway. I tap-dance. I click and turn. I start to sing.

" I'll help you with the dishes, " Mom says to my aunt.

I go into my cartwheel. I stand up for applause. Everyone has left. I decide to skip the jokes.

I'm giving up. I tried three plans. I tried being different. I tried being mysterious. I tried being lively. None of them worked. I guess nobody will ever be interested in me.

Billy Michaels comes over. "Why did you wear that funny hat the other day?" he asks. I don't answer. He sits down and opens his lunch box. He takes out a pickle.

"Billy," I say. "How come every day you have pickles in your lunch box?"

Billy smiles. "So you saw," he says.

"Sure," I say. "Who hasn't?"

"Well, maybe they have," Billy said. "But nobody has ever asked me about them before."

"Oh," I say. "Well, why do you have pickles?"

"My dad's a pickle-maker," he says.

"Really?" I say.

"Yes. And I know how to make them, too."

"Wow, could you teach me how?"

"Yes," he says.

Billy and I are making pickles. We're asking each other lots of questions. I think he's interesting. He thinks about a lot of things, just like me. He wonders why his cat's tongue is so scratchy. He wonders why some plants grow from seeds and some don't.

Billy wonders why I never asked him about his pickles before. I wonder why I never asked him before, too.

I'm sure glad I finally did.

LIFE SKILL: Shopping List

Rachel and Billy began a friendship over Billy's pickles. They had fun making pickles together. But before they could make the pickles, they had to be sure they had all the things they needed. They looked at the beginning of the pickle recipe. Everything they needed was written there. They had to go to the store to buy some of the things.

Look at this recipe. On your paper, make a shopping list. List all the things you will need to buy. Do you need to buy bread? Do you need to buy dill?

HOW TO MAKE PICKLES

What You Need:

6 cucumbers	1/4 cup of salt
2 small sprigs of dill	2 peppercorns
2 buds of garlic	2 cloves
1 gallon of hot water	1 bay leaf
1 cup of vinegar	

What You Do:

Wash and dry the cucumbers. Next, put a sprig of dill, one bud of garlic, one peppercorn, one clove, and the bay leaf into a big jar. Then add the cucumbers. Now put the rest of the dill, garlic, peppercorn, and clove on top of the cucumbers.

In a bowl, mix the water, salt, and vinegar. This mixture is called *brine.* Stir the mixture well. Next, add the brine to the cucumbers. Put a plate on top of the brine and cucumbers. The plate will help keep the cucumbers under the brine.

Let the cucumbers soak in the brine. In a few days, you will see some foam at the top of the brine. Be sure to take this foam off every day.

The pickles will be ready in two to four weeks.

CHECKPOINT

Write each sentence using the correct word.

been   mysterious   dye   suit   peacocks   pickle

1. A _____ man was sneaking around the village.

2. I love to eat a _____ with my lunch every day.

3. Matching slacks and coat are called a _____.

4. Stephen doesn't think _____ are ugly birds.

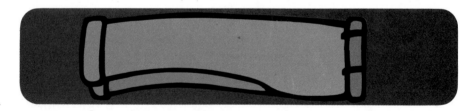

Write the best answer to each question.

Felipe sees a new girl come into class. He remembers his first day at school. He decides to go across the room and say hello. As he reaches the new girl's desk, he smiles.

5. What is Felipe like?

    a. foolish

    b. friendly

    c. funny

6. Why does Felipe cross the room?

    a. He knows he left his books on someone's desk.

    b. He knows it's time to sit down.

    c. He knows what it's like on the first day of school.

Write the best answer to each question.

Decoding:
Vowel *a;*
Prefixes *re-, un-*

The alarm rang, catching Lin's attention. She uncovered her head, moaned, and looked at the clock. It was unwise to stay in bed much longer. She had to rejoin the workers at the barn today. They were going to refit the barn door. Lin jumped up, put on her clothes, and left the room. She hoped there would be no questions about her unmade bed.

7. What woke Lin up?

    a. a lamb outside her window

    b. a turkey in the yard

    c. an alarm in her room

8. Why was it unwise for Lin to stay in bed?

    a. She wanted to remake her bed.

    b. She had to rejoin the workers in the barn.

    c. She was going to the park.

My great corn plants,
Among them I walk,
I speak to them,
They hold out their hands to me.

Navajo song

156

Corn Is Maize

Aliki

This is a kernel of corn.

It is a corn seed.

Kernels of corn are planted in a small hill of good earth. The sun shines down on them. Spring rains water the earth. The hard seeds grow soft and sprout.

A leaf sprouts, and a stalk begins to grow. More leaves come out. A corn stalk shoots up fast.

Now it is the middle of the summer. The corn plant is taller than a farmer. Husks have started to sprout. A husk is a bunch of leaves. The husk is tightly wrapped around strands of silk. A kernel of corn will grow at the end of each strand.

As the corn grows, the silk changes color. The silk turns from a light yellow to dark red to brown.

Just before the silk turns brown, it is time to pick the corn from the stalk. The corn is unwrapped. The husks and the silk are pulled away. The sweet ear of corn is ready to cook and eat.

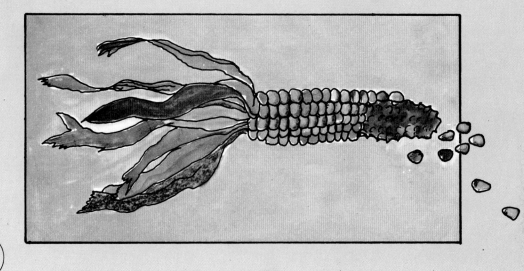

Thousands of years ago, the people of America learned how to grow corn. When Columbus landed in America, he saw that the first Americans were good farmers. Corn was one of their main crops. Columbus called these people "Indians."

The first Americans ate corn many ways. Some of it they ate fresh. They ate corn on the cob. They cooked baby corn in the husks. They ate the ears whole.

The first Americans dried most of the corn. They stored it for the long winter ahead. They saved some of the corn for seed. They ground the rest into meal on a flat stone. They ate the meal dry or cooked it into mush. They made corn meal bread and pancakes. They popped corn, too.

Corn was the first Americans' main food. They needed it to live.

Columbus returned home. He told about the people of America. He spoke of the corn they grew.

He called corn "maize." Maize sounded like the name the first Americans had used.

When the Pilgrims landed in America, maize saved their lives. The first Americans gave them maize to eat. They showed the Pilgrims how to plant the maize.

The Pilgrims called maize "Indian corn." Americans still call maize "corn."

The Pilgrims learned other things about corn from the first Americans. They made soft beds with corn husks. They burned corn cobs in fires. They made toys from corn, too.

Today farmers all over the world grow corn. There are many kinds of corn. We eat sweet corn. Other kinds are used to feed animals and to make things.

Here are some things made from corn:

| corn flour | cornmeal | cornstarch |
| baby powder | glue | soap |

SOCIAL STUDIES READING: What's It All About?

The first Americans knew a lot about growing corn. Today corn is still an important food. On the next page you will learn more about how corn grows.

TAKE A FIRST LOOK

What do you see on the next page? What does the map show you? What do you think you will be reading about?

FIND THE KEY IDEAS

The title of the story is "Corn Growing." What is the title of the map? How do the map and the story go together?

READ CAREFULLY

Now read the story on the next page. How do machines help the farmer? How do trucks help the farmer? Look closely at the map. Does corn grow where you live?

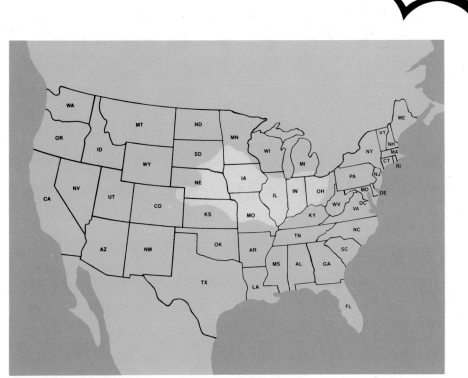

The gold part shows where many corn farms are.

CORN GROWING

Much corn grows on big farms. The map shows where these big farms are. This is how a corn farm works: First, the farmer gets the soil ready. Then a machine puts corn seeds in the soil. When the corn is ripe, people use machines to pick the corn. The farmer pays the people who run the machines.

Trucks take the corn away to be stored. Then some of the corn is taken to markets and sold. One kind of corn is used to feed animals. Another kind of corn is used to make other foods. What foods do you like to eat that are made from corn?

The Turnip

Slavic Folktale retold by Janina Domanska

Grandfather planted a turnip in the garden. Grandmother watered it every day. The turnip got bigger and bigger. "My turnip is beautiful!" cried Grandfather.

"Ho! Ho!" laughed Grandmother. "Your turnip! It's my turnip. Didn't I water it every day?"

"Ho! Ho!" shouted Grandfather. "I planted it, didn't I? So it's my turnip."

The turnip grew huge. One morning, Grandmother said, "I'll pull that turnip before the birds eat it."

She ran to the garden. She pulled and pulled until she couldn't pull any more. The turnip did not move. "This turnip weighs a ton!" Grandmother said.

164

The next morning, Grandfather decided to pull the turnip. "It's so big," he thought. "The neighbor's goat might start eating it." So Grandfather pulled and pulled until he couldn't pull any more. The turnip did not move. "This turnip weighs a ton!" Grandfather said.

Then Grandfather called Grandmother to help him pull the turnip. Grandmother came running.

"We will pull OUR turnip!" she cried. So they pulled together. They pulled and pulled until they were both out of breath. The turnip did not move.

Grandfather wiped the sweat from his brow. "Let's call Micky to help us," he said.

Micky, their grandson, came, and they all pulled. They puffed and they pulled until they couldn't pull any more. The turnip did not move.

"Get the dog to help," said Grandfather when he had his breath back.

The dog came and pulled at Micky. They all pulled and pulled and pulled until they couldn't pull any more. The turnip did not move.

The cat saw them all pulling and panting. She came and pulled behind the dog. They all pulled and pulled and puffed and pulled. The turnip did not move.

Then the geese came to help. They made a goose chain, and they pulled with the others. They all pulled and pulled and pulled. The turnip did not move.

"This turnip is laughing at us!" shouted Grandfather. He wiped the sweat from his brow. "Get the rooster and the hen. They can pull," he said.

The rooster and the hen came and pulled behind the geese. "Now all together!" shouted Grandfather. "One . . . two . . . three . . . PULL!"

They pulled and they puffed. They pulled and pulled. The turnip did not move.

Now only the pig was not pulling. He was a very big, fat pig. Grandmother shouted, "Get that pig! Make him pull with us!"

So the pig came and pulled at the hen.

"All together now," shouted Grandmother. "One . . . two . . . three . . . PULL!" They pulled and they panted. They pulled and pulled and pulled. The turnip did not move.

Grandfather wiped the sweat from his brow. "No old turnip is going to beat us," he growled. " We will try again. Now all together." So everyone got ready to pull.

The pig took a deep breath. The rooster flapped his wings. The geese honked. Grandfather counted, "One . . . two . . . three . . . PULL!"

They all pulled and pulled and pulled. Soon they were all out of breath. The turnip did not move.

Grandfather wiped some more sweat from his brow. "We will try once more. All of you pull. That means you!" he shouted at the pig.

The pig took such a deep breath that he nearly blew the curl out of his tail. This time he got ready to pull with the others.

Grandmother was about to give the signal for them all to pull at the turnip. Just then a bird flew down to help. She pulled at the pig's tail. "Now all together!" cried Grandmother. They all pulled with all their might. They pulled and pulled and pulled.

At once there was a loud noise. The turnip came out of the ground so fast that they all fell down.

"Oh, my!" cried the bird. "Look what I have done." She flew away to her tall tree. From there, she looked at them all lying flat on the grass.

Grandfather sat hugging the huge turnip in his arms.

The Robbers and the Fig Tree

adapted by Genie Iverson from a Mexican folktale

Players

TÍA CARMEN

TÍO TOMÁS

SARITA, their niece

BIG ROBBER

MIDDLE ROBBER

SMALL ROBBER

STORYTELLER

Act One

STORYTELLER: Tomás, Carmen, and their niece Sarita own a large farm. In the garden is a beautiful green fig tree. Now it is summer. The figs are getting ripe. Tomás goes outside to pick figs. Carmen and Sarita are talking together near the back door.

TÍA CARMEN: What can be keeping Tío Tomás?
(*The door opens, and Tomás enters. He is carrying an empty basket.*)

TÍO TOMÁS: (*He shakes his head.*) Who would do such a thing? Who would do such a bad thing?

TÍA CARMEN: What are you talking about?

TÍO TOMÁS: Robbers came into our garden last night. They took some figs. (*He slams his empty basket down on the table.*)

SARITA: Did they steal all the figs?

TÍO TOMÁS: They took all the ripe ones. Tonight I won't go to bed. I'll stay outside and keep watch. If they come back again, I'll be waiting.

173

TÍA CARMEN:	You'll be tired from work. Can you stay awake?
TÍO TOMÁS:	I have to.
SARITA:	(*She takes her uncle's hand.*) I'll help. You and I will keep watch together.

Act Two

STORYTELLER:	That night, Tío Tomás and Sarita sit together in the dark.
SARITA:	(*yawning*) Do you see anything, Tío?
TÍO TOMÁS:	I see only the leaves shining in the light of the moon. Rest, little one.
SARITA:	(*She lays her head on her arms.*) I'll rest, Tío, but I won't shut my eyes.
TÍO TOMÁS:	(*in a sleepy voice*) Maybe those robbers won't even come. Maybe our figs will be safe.

(*His head drops down, and he sleeps.*)

(*Three robbers enter. They tiptoe to the tree. Then they see Tomás and Sarita.*)

SMALL ROBBER: (*whispering*) Let's get out of here!

BIG ROBBER: (*whispering*) Wait! It's only Tomás and his niece. They're asleep.

MIDDLE ROBBER: Then why are we standing around?

ROBBERS: (*They chant softly.*)

Tiptoe. Tiptoe.

Shake the tree.

Figs for you,

And figs for me.

SMALL ROBBER: (*He whispers the last line to himself.*) Figs for me.

STORYTELLER: The robbers eat some figs. They stuff their bags with figs. Then they tiptoe away.

Act Three

STORYTELLER: The next night, Sarita and her uncle watched the fig tree again. Sarita brought their old dog, Amiga. She thought Amiga would be a good watchdog. But when Sarita and Tomás fell asleep, so did Amiga. Amiga did not bark when the robbers came. The next night, Tomás tied small bells to the branches of the tree. He knew that the robbers would shake the tree to get the figs. He thought the ringing of the bells would wake him. But the bells made sweet music. Tomás and Sarita went on sleeping. Tonight the family is sitting in the kitchen. Dinner is just over.

TÍO TOMÁS: (*He shakes his head sadly.*) Night after night, those robbers come. Night after night, we fall asleep and don't catch them. Soon we won't have any figs left. (*He leans on the table and sighs.*)

TÍA CARMEN: Tomás, Sarita, you have tried so hard. Still, we must not give up. (*She pushes her chair back.*) I have an idea.

SARITA: What's your idea, Tía Carmen?

TÍO TOMÁS: (*sighing*) We've already tried everything.

177

TÍA CARMEN: I know one idea we haven't tried. Sarita, go bring me that big pail of tar and our broom. (*Sarita leaves. Soon Sarita comes back. She hands her aunt the tar and the broom.*)

TÍA CARMEN: Just what we need, something sticky for tricky robbers.

SARITA: What do you mean?
(*Tía Carmen goes to the door with the tar and the broom.*)

TÍA CARMEN: Tonight you will sleep in nice, soft beds. I will watch the fig tree. (*She goes out, closing the door behind her.*)

Act Four

STORYTELLER: Tía Carmen spreads sticky tar on the trunk and branches of the fig tree. Then she lies down to rest. Soon she sleeps. Her broom and empty pail lie on the ground next to her. As time passes, the moon climbs high into the sky. (*Three robbers enter on tiptoe, chanting softly.*)

ROBBERS: Tiptoe. Tiptoe.
Shake the tree.
Figs for you,
And figs for me.

SMALL ROBBER: (*He whispers the last line again, softly.*) Figs for me.

MIDDLE ROBBER: Look! Here is Carmen. (*He tiptoes over to her.*) She's asleep, just as the others were.

BIG ROBBER: Well, when people work hard all day, they sleep all night long.

SMALL ROBBER: (*softly*) No wonder we don't need to sleep at night.

(*The robbers tiptoe to the fig tree. Small Robber and Middle Robber grab the tree. Big Robber waits for the ripe figs to drop.*)

BIG ROBBER: Well, hurry. Shake down some figs.

MIDDLE ROBBER: I can't. I'm stuck.

SMALL ROBBER: I am, too.

BIG ROBBER: Can't you two do anything right? (*He wraps his arms around the tree trunk.*) You grab the tree like this. Oh! Help!

(*Tía Carmen sits up. Tío Tomás and Sarita come from the house.*)

TÍO TOMÁS: What's all the noise?

SARITA: You trapped the robbers, Tía Carmen!

MIDDLE ROBBER: Set us free, please. We'll never steal any figs again.

BIG ROBBER: We'll pay you for the figs we ate, too. We'll even work for you.

SMALL ROBBER: Yes, we'll even work for you.

STORYTELLER: And so they did. Each day the three men worked hard. Each day they pulled weeds. Each day they carried pails of water to the corn. Each night the three men were tired from their day of hard work. They lay under the fig tree and fell asleep. Of course, Tío Tomás, Tía Carmen, and Sarita could sleep in peace, too. And everyone had figs to eat.

181

CHECKPOINT

Write the word that does not belong with the others.

1. kernel   stalk   leaf   tiptoes

2. grandmother   turnip   grandfather   grandson

3. enter   farmer   painter   tailor

4. duck   suit   rooster   goose

Write the best answer to each question.

Grandfather is watching Ann fish. The sun is behind a cloud. The air is still. All at once, Ann feels a pull on her line. "I've got a nibble, Grandfather!" she shouts. Ann starts pulling in her line.

5. Why does Ann start pulling in her line?

a. The sun is behind a cloud.

b. Ann feels a pull on her line.

c. Grandfather hears Ann shout.

Ken was out working in the garden. The sky turned dark. It started to rain. Ken knew he would get wet if he stayed outside. Ken ran inside.

6. Why did Ken run inside?

    a. Ken liked working in the garden.

    b. Ken's mother called him.

    c. Ken knew he would get wet.

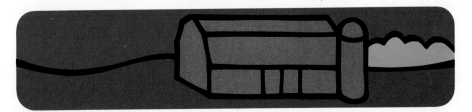

Write the best answer to each question.

Decoding:
Vowel *ei*,
Consonant *dg(e)*

Dan and Bill were hiding together in the barn. "Now's the time to act," whispered Dan. "Grab the reins and get going!" Bill jumped down from the ledge and grabbed the reins. "I'll meet you up on the ridge at eight," he said.

7. Where were Dan and Bill hiding?

    a. up on the ridge

    b. on a ledge in the barn

    c. in a corn field

8. What did Bill grab?

    a. the barn door

    b. Dan's hand

    c. the reins

Don't Sne

Good detectives look for clues. Clues can be hard to find. Any clue—no matter how small—is nothing to sneeze at!

Things don't stay lost around Nate. He spots all the clues. Kate finds the answer to a riddle. She'll tell you the secret if your name's not Wally!

Be a detective, too! Look at your fingers. They have "tips" to give you. Add the clues together. What do you have? Another puzzle!

Don't give up! Keep looking for clues. Watch out! There's mud ahead . . . and it's wonderful. Let it ooze all over. It might lead to a mess of an adventure!

Stand back, way back. It's OK to sneeze now. Just don't blow the clues away!

eze Now

185

Nate the Great
and the
Lost List

Marjorie Weinman Sharmat

I, Nate the Great, am a busy detective. One morning I was not busy. I was on my vacation. I was sitting under a tree with my dog, Sludge, and a pancake. Sludge needed a vacation, too.

My friend Claude came into the yard. I knew that he had lost something. That's the way Claude was.

"I lost my way to your house," he said. "And then I found it."

"What else did you lose?" I asked.

"I lost the grocery list I was bringing to the store. Can you help me find it?"

"I, Nate the Great, am on my vacation," I said.

"When will your vacation be over?"

"At lunch," I answered.

"I need the list before lunch," Claude said.

"Very well. I, Nate the Great, will take your case. Tell me. What did you have to buy?"

"If I could remember, I wouldn't need the list," Claude said.

"Good thinking," I said.

"Can you remember any of the list?" I asked.

"Yes," Claude said. "I remember salt, milk, butter, flour, sugar, and tuna fish."

"Now, tell me," I said. "Where did you lose the list?"

"If I knew, I could find it," Claude said.

"You can't be sure of that," I said. "What streets did you walk on?"

"I'm not sure," Claude said. "I lost my way a few times."

"Then I, Nate the Great, know what to do," I said. "I will draw a map. It will have every street between your house and the grocery store.

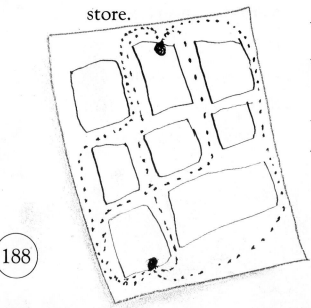

We will look there."

Sludge and I got up. Our vacation was over.

I got a piece of paper. I drew a map on the paper.

Claude said, "I will walk with you."

We walked between Claude's house and the grocery store. Then we walked between the grocery store and Claude's house. Sludge sniffed, but we could not find the list.

"Maybe it blew away," I said. I dropped the map to the ground.

"What are you doing?" Claude asked.

"I dropped the map," I answered. "The way it goes will show us where the wind is blowing. Maybe your list blew the same way."

The map blew over to Rosa's house.

"I will go to Rosa's house," I said. "I will ask her if she has seen your list."

Sludge and I went to Rosa's house. Rosa opened the door. She looked strange and white. She was covered with flour. Sludge sniffed hard. I sniffed hard. Rosa smelled great. She was making pancakes!

We walked in. Rosa's four black cats were there. Today they were white, too.

"I am making cat pancakes from a new recipe," Rosa said. "I am having a cat pancake party this morning."

"I would like to taste cat pancakes," I said.

"You are not a cat," Rosa said.

"I would like to taste them anyway," I said. "A pancake is a pancake."

Rosa and I sat down. I ate a pancake. It had a fishy taste. I ate another. It tasted even more fishy.

"I am looking for Claude's grocery list," I said. "I think the wind blew it to your house. Have you seen it?"

"I haven't seen a grocery list," Rosa said.

I got up. "Thank you for your help and your pancakes," I said.

Sludge and I walked to Claude's house. Claude was home. He was not lost. It was a good sign.

"I, Nate the Great, have not found your list," I said. "Can you remember anything else you had to buy?"

"How will that help you find the list?" Claude asked.

"You'll see," I said.

"I remember! I remember two more things," Claude said. "Eggs and baking powder were on the list."

"Very good," I said.

"Can you find the list before lunch?" Claude asked.

"I hope so," I said. "Come to my house around twelve."

Sludge and I walked home slowly. This was a hard case to solve.

At home I made myself some pancakes. I mixed eggs, flour, salt, baking powder, milk, butter, and sugar together. Then I cooked them.

I gave Sludge a bone. I ate and thought. I thought about the grocery list. I thought about Rosa and her fishy cat pancakes. I put ideas together. I took them apart.

Then I had a big idea. I knew I must go back to Rosa's house.

Sludge and I walked quickly to Rosa's house. I said hello to Rosa and to more cats than I could count.

"I came to talk about your cat pancakes," I said.

"Would you like more?" Rosa asked.

"I would like to see your recipe," I said.

"Here it is," Rosa said.

"Tell me, where did you get this recipe?" I asked.

"I found it today," Rosa said.

"You found it!" I said. "Did you find it near your house?"

"Yes," Rosa said. "How did you know that?"

"I have something to tell you," I said. "I, Nate the Great, say that your cat pancake recipe is Claude's grocery list."

I read the recipe.

" Salt. Milk. Butter. Flour. Tuna fish. Eggs. Baking powder. Sugar. Salmon. Liver."

"Oh," Rosa said. "When I found the paper, I thought it was a cat pancake recipe."

"Yes," I said. "When you saw the grocery list, you thought it was what you wanted. You wanted a cat pancake recipe."

"I, Nate the Great, solved the case when I was making pancakes," I said. "I mixed eggs, flour, salt, baking powder, milk, butter, and sugar. Claude had told me they were on his list. The other thing he remembered he had to buy was tuna fish. Cats like tuna fish. So, I came up with cat pancakes!"

"Oh," Rosa said. "Well, Claude can have his paper back. I will keep the recipe in my head."

"That is a good place for it," I said. "It cannot blow away."

Sludge and I went home with the list. The case was solved.

It is now after twelve. Here comes Claude. I am glad the case is over. I, Nate the Great, have something important to do.

I, Nate the Great, am going to go back to my vacation.

Kate's Secret Riddle Book

Sid Fleischman

Wally lives across the street. On Saturday he rang our bell.

"Let me in, Jimmy," he said to my brother.

"No," Jimmy said. "My sister is sick."

"I want to tell her a riddle," said Wally. He grinned. "It will make her laugh."

Jimmy hadn't been able to make me laugh all week.

"Do you want to hear a riddle?" Wally asked me.

"No," I said.

"It's a funny riddle," said Wally.

"Well, OK." I nodded.

"Ready?" asked Wally.

"Here's the riddle: Bulldozer!"

197

I said, "That's not a riddle!"

"It's the answer to one," said Wally. He laughed. "You've got to think of the question. That's the funny part!"

"I feel sick," I said.

"You are sick," Jimmy pointed out.

"I feel sicker," I groaned. "Wally will never tell us the riddle."

"Maybe someone knows it," Jimmy said.

The next day I was well. On my way to the grocery store, I met the mail carrier.

"Do you know any riddles, Mr. Hunt?" I asked.

Mr. Hunt scratched his head. "What did the fly say when it fell into butter?"

"Bulldozer," I answered.

"No," he said. "'Look! I'm a butterfly.'"

At the grocery store, I asked Mrs. Mitchell if she knew any riddles.

"Let me think," said Mrs. Mitchell. "If you put a clock in a beehive, what time would it be?"

"I give up," I said.

"Why, it would be hive o'clock," Mrs. Mitchell said with a smile.

I helped Mr. List carry his bags out of the grocery store. "Do you know any riddles, Mr. List?" I asked.

"Of course I do," he answered. "If ducks say 'Quack, quack' when they walk, what do they say when they run?"

"Bulldozer?" I asked.

"They say 'Quick! Quick!'" he answered.

Maybe Wally had made up that answer, I thought. Still, it gave me an idea.

I ran back to the store and got a small school pad. I would write down all the riddles before I forgot any. Just about everyone I met had a riddle to tell.

The book was nearly full when I visited Mr. Cross. He owned a farm.

"Oh, I know a riddle," Mr. Cross said. "What side of a house gets the most rain?"

"I don't know, Mr. Cross," I said sadly.

"The outside," he said with a laugh.

I wrote the riddle down. Just then I saw Mr. Cross's bull sleeping in the field.

Mr. Cross looked at the bull and sighed. "That lazy bull dozes all day," he said. "I never saw an animal sleep so much."

I gave a shout. I knew the question to Wally's riddle!

I wrote the riddle in the book. On the cover I printed KATE'S SECRET RIDDLE BOOK. Then I ran home as fast as I could. I stood outside Wally's house and laughed hard. I wanted Wally to hear me. Soon Wally came to the window.

"What are you laughing at?" he asked.

"Your riddle," I answered. "Bulldozer." I giggled. "Wally, that's the funniest riddle in the whole world."

"It is?" Wally said.

"I can't stop laughing," I said.

"Tell me the first part," begged Wally.

"Oh, you know it," I teased.

Wally said, "No, I don't. I just made up that answer to tease you. I really don't know the question."

"You're just pretending," I laughed. "Oh, the riddle is so funny. Don't worry. Jimmy and I will keep it a secret."

"Come on and tell me," Wally said.

"You're looking kind of sick, Wally," I said. "You'd better go home to bed. As for me, I'm feeling much better."

I held up my secret riddle book and read the last riddle again.

What do you call
a sleeping bull?

Bulldozer

(Don't tell Wally.)

STUDY SKILL: Classification

Kate and Nate were good detectives. They knew how to find clues. Fingerprints can be good clues. Every person in the world has different fingerprints. Your fingerprints tell that you are you!

There are three kinds of fingerprints. They are the arch, the loop, and the whorl.

| Arch | Loop | Whorl |

The arch bends a little bit. The loop looks like a hairpin. The whorl goes round and round like a spinning top. Look closely at the different kinds of fingerprints.

What kinds of fingerprints do you have? To find out, you will need some clear tape. Put your fingertips on the sticky side of the tape. Do one finger at a time. Pull the tape off your fingers. Hold the tape up to a light. Now you can see your fingerprints. What kinds of fingerprints do you have? What kinds of fingerprints do your friends have?

FINGERPRINTS

My Friends	Arch	Loop	Whorl
Emily	X		
Chu Sun			X
Ann		X	
Hank		X	

You can make a chart of your friend's fingerprint. Pick one finger. Make a fingerprint. On your paper, make a chart like this one. Fill in your friend's name. Put a mark under the kind of fingerprint your friend has. You can do this with lots of friends!

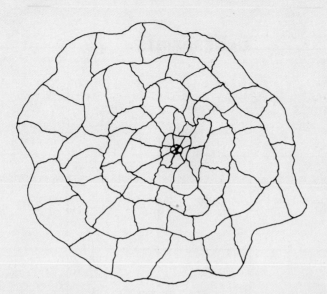

PUZZLE

Map of a city with streets meeting at center?
Net to catch people jumping
from a burning building?
Spider's web?
Burner on an electric stove?
Fingerprint?
No.
Frozen puddle after a hit by a rock.

Robert Froman

How to Be a Nature Detective

Millicent Selsam

"What happened here?" a detective asks.
"Who was here? Where did someone go?" A
detective has many ways to find out.

One way to find out is to look for the
marks that someone or something has made.
Fingerprints, footprints, and tracks made by
tires are marks. These things are clues. Clues
help a detective answer these questions:

What happened?

Who was here?

Where did someone go?

You can be a detective, too. You can be a nature detective. Nature detectives find tracks and clues. Nature detectives answer these questions:

What animal walked here?

Where did it go?

What did it do?

What did it eat?

You can find tracks in many places. You can find tracks in mud, in snow, in sand, and in dust. You can even find them on the sidewalk or on the floor. Wet feet or muddy paws can make a track anywhere.

Here is a job for a nature detective:

There is a cat. There is a dog. There is a dish for the cat. There is a dish for the dog. The cat's dish had milk in it. The dog's dish had meat in it.

Who drank the milk? Who ate the meat? Look at the tracks and see.

Look at the tracks that go to the cat's dish. They were made by an animal that walks on four feet. You can see claw marks in front. A cat has four feet and claws. But so does a dog. Who went to the cat's dish? We still don't know.

Let's look for more clues.

Now look at the tracks that go to the dog's dish. No claw marks!

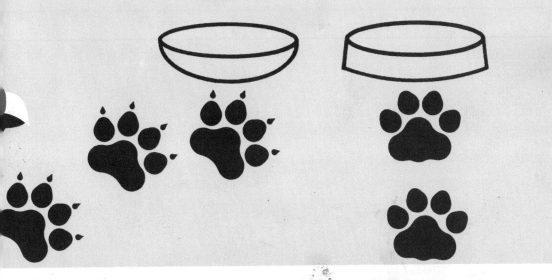

Did you ever watch a cat walk? The tracks of a cat's back feet fall right on the tracks of its front feet. So its footprints are one behind the other, in one line. They look like the footprints of an animal with only two legs.

A cat pulls its claws in when it walks. That is why it does not leave claw marks.

Now do you know who drank the milk? (THE DOG!) Who ate the meat? (THE CAT!)

A fox makes tracks in one line, just as a cat does. But fox tracks have claw marks, just like a dog's. You may see fox tracks if you walk through a snowy woods.

What kind of footprints will a rabbit make? You can see that a rabbit has little front paws and big back feet.

The little front paws will make little paw prints. The big back feet will make big tracks.

Here is another job for a nature detective: Who went lickety-split across the snow?

A rabbit did. Which way did it go? Did it go to the tree? Did it go away from the tree?

The rabbit seems to have gone to the tree. Do you agree? You can see the marks of the front paws ahead of the big back feet.

Do you know how a rabbit jumps? Look at the tracks.

When a rabbit jumps, it puts its big back feet ahead of its front paws.

What happened here on a snowy day?

You can see the rabbit tracks in the snow. You know that the tracks are going away from the tree.

All at once, the rabbit tracks are far apart. That means the rabbit began to take big jumps. It was in a hurry. Why?

Do you see those tracks coming out of the woods? Those footprints have claw marks like a dog's. But they are in one line, like the tracks of a cat. Who could have made those tracks? There is only one answer. (a fox)

Now you know why the rabbit was in a hurry!

Did the fox catch the rabbit? Look again at the picture on page 211. What do you think?

Tracks are good clues for a nature detective.
There are other clues, too. A nature detective
learns to look and listen, and to smell.

A detective can find clues in a backyard, in
the woods, or in a city park.

Who lives here?
Who ate here?
Who went by?
Do you know who made these tracks?
Follow the tracks and see.

Written in Sand

Some people read tracks
like they'd read a story.
(The story is
true.
It's written
in sand.)

Tracks tell
if a mouse
ran fast or slow
and if it carried
something
as it went along.

They tell if it
suddenly
stopped
in fear

and then jumped back
behind a weed
and hid,
quiet
as any stone.

Tracks tell
everything
that happens.
They name
everyone
who passes.

Byrd Baylor

215

CHECKPOINT

Write each sentence using the correct word.

1. The detective found a secret clue that helped him _____ the mystery.

buy   solve   powder

2. I had a wonderful _____ fishing for tuna.

sugar   powder   vacation

3. In science we read about _____.

nature   recipes   riddle

4. I had a lot of letters in the _____ today.

milk   secret   mail

Write the best answer to each question.

Jane opened the door and walked inside. She passed by rows and rows of cans. She looked at her list of foods. She picked up a can of dog food and took it to a woman. The woman put the can in a bag. Then Jane gave the woman some coins and left.

5. Where was Jane?

    a. in a bulldozer

    b. at work

    c. at the grocery store

6. What kind of pet does Jane have?

    a. a bird

    b. a fish

    c. a dog

Write the best answer to each question.

Neil lay on the bed looking up at the ceiling. He wondered just what he should do today. All at once, he was seized by a pair of hands. "Outside with you! Go lie under the bushes!" Neil was a bulldog, you see!

7. What was Neil looking at?

    a. the bed

    b. the bushes

    c. the ceiling

8. What seized Neil?

    a. a bulldog

    b. a pair of hands

    c. the wind

Go with the poem.
Hang glide
above new landscape
into other weather.

Sail the poem.
Lift.
Drift over treetops
and towers.

Loop with the poem.
Swoop, dip.
Land.
Where?
Trust the poem.

Lilian Moore

Pea Soup
and Sea Serpents

William E. Schroder

Norton and Atherton decided to hunt for sea serpents.

"We will need a rope to tie it up, should we catch one," said Atherton.

"We will need a pail to carry it in," said Norton.

"If it is not too large," said Atherton.

"How big could it be if it lives in a pond?" asked Norton.

"It is foggy," said Atherton.

"Like pea soup," said Norton.

"That will make it easier to take the serpent by surprise," said Atherton.

Norton said, "My glasses are getting all foggy, too."

"Do you see any sea serpents?" asked Norton.

"I believe they are very shy beasts," said Atherton.

"I see," said Norton.

"We will take out the boat," said Atherton.

"Do you know much about boats?" asked Norton.

"Not a great deal," said Atherton.

"Neither do I," said Norton.

"Then we should put on the life jackets," said Atherton.

"Yes," said Norton.

"How far are we from shore?" asked Norton.

"I cannot see the shore," answered Atherton.

"Neither can I," said Norton. "I can barely see the water. It really is quiet."

"That is because there is nobody about today," said Atherton.

"The boat is rocking," said Norton.

"The sea is getting choppy," said Atherton. "It is getting rough."

"Maybe there is a storm coming up," said Norton.

"Man overboard!" said Atherton.

"Men overboard!" said Norton.

"At least the water is not cold," said Norton.

"I think we should swim to shore," said Atherton.

"Where is it?" asked Norton.

"Stay near me so you do not get lost," said Atherton.

"Where are you?" asked Norton.

"Here I am," said Atherton.

"I am being lifted out of the water," said Norton.

"Perhaps our boat has come up under us," said Atherton.

"Whatever is under me does not feel like a boat," said Norton.

"What else could it be?" asked Atherton.

"We are moving, if I am not greatly mistaken," said Norton.

"Perhaps there is a strong wind pushing us," said Atherton.

"Perhaps," said Norton.

"I wonder where we are headed," said Norton.

"To shore, I hope," said Atherton.

"I hope so, too," said Norton.

"That was a rough landing," said Atherton.

"Very rough," said Norton.

"Are you all right?" asked Atherton.

"I am all right," said Norton. "I wonder if the boat is hurt."

"I cannot see the boat," said Norton.

"Neither can I," said Atherton. "Perhaps we should go home and change into dry clothes."

"Perhaps we will find a sea serpent another time," said Atherton.

"When it is less foggy," added Norton.

"If there are any to find in a pond," said Atherton. He sneezed.

How Mud Was Discovered

Oliver G. Selfridge

Caroline lived in a very special town. The whole town was very clean. It was a dirtless town. There was no dirt anywhere. You would think that everyone would be very happy. Not everyone was.

Caroline was unhappy. She wanted to hide so birds and animals would not see her in the woods. Then she could watch them. She needed something to make her clothes, face, hands, and hair dirty. But there was no dirt to be found anywhere.

Caroline's parents were *very* sad. The family had just got a beautiful new washing machine. But the machine was useless. There were never any dirty clothes to put in it. What could they wash?

Caroline had a brother named Ethan. He wasn't really happy or unhappy. He was looking for a way to make mud pies. Of course, there wasn't any such thing as mud in their town. There wasn't any dirt. Ethan and Caroline were outside looking under trees and by the stream. But there wasn't any mud at all.

They sat next to the stream. They watched the ripples playing with each other and going off down the stream. One ripple was trapped by a rock below the water.

Caroline reached into the water. "I think I will give that ripple some help," she said. She took the rock out from under the ripple.

"There it goes!" shouted Caroline. She squeezed the rock in her hand. The rock broke open with a little "tssss." Caroline's fingers were covered with mud. It was the first mud that they had ever seen.

"What is that?" asked Ethan. He reached out and touched her hand. His hands became covered with mud, too.

"I'm not sure," said Caroline. "I think it is mud. Look." She touched the tip of her nose. Of course, it became covered with mud. Ethan laughed and laughed.

"Put some on *your* nose," said Caroline. "Then I can see how it looks. It's very hard to see mine unless I cross my eyes."

Ethan gave himself two more eyebrows made of mud and a large mud mustache. Caroline laughed and laughed. She made a mud spot in the middle of her forehead.

Ethan looked at his right hand. It was covered with mud. He brought his hand up to his shirt. He put it on flat. He took his hand away. There was a large, muddy hand on his shirt.

"Oh, Ethan," Caroline said. "You have made your shirt wonderfully dirty." Caroline made her shoes and socks wonderfully dirty, too. "Let's go home and show Mother."

"We aren't done yet," he said.

In a little while, they walked home. They went to the back door of their house. They rang the bell. They were covered with mud from head to foot. There were some holes in the mud where their eyes, noses, and mouths were.

231

Soon their mother came to the door. She opened it and stared at those two large piles of mud. She had never seen them before. When she saw that they were Caroline and Ethan, she gave a cry of joy.

" Oh, children, how wonderful ! How wonderfully dirty you are ! I will call your father so that he can see you, too. Come hug me, and I'll become all muddy, too."

So Caroline and Ethan hugged their mother and their father. Soon they were all covered with mud from hair to shoes.

"I like the feel of mud. But I don't like the taste of mud, " said their father. He had forgotten to leave a hole for his mouth.

"I think I will wipe my hands before I cook dinner," said their mother.

" Tomorrow you must change your clothes," said their father. "I will take all the dirty ones. I will put them in the beautiful new washing machine. I will get them clean."

Their parents were very happy.

Caroline and Ethan said they would get muddy whenever they felt like it. Then their parents could use their new washing machine every day.

That is only one story about how mud was discovered in Caroline's town. If you think of a better story, write it down. Send it to us.

All About Mud

Oliver G. Selfridge

Mud is really dirt mixed with water. But what kind of dirt do you use? Lots of kinds, but not every kind of dirt will do. You can't use the dirt on a dirty shirt you were wearing when you oiled your bike. You can't use the dirt from a vacuum cleaner to make mud. But you can use most dirt that you find on the ground.

A good place to look for mud is in your garden after a good rain. If it hasn't been raining, make your own rain with the hose. Spray water right in the dirt. Then mix the dirt with the water. Squishing it with your fingers or toes is the best way to mix it.

You may happen to live where there is a lot of water and not very much dirt, as on a boat. Get some dirt and put it in a pail. Pour water into the pail. If you don't use enough water, you will have a mix that is stiff, called "wet dirt." That is not the same thing as mud at all. You'll need to add more water at once.

If you don't use enough dirt, you will have a mix called "dirty water." This is a kind of mud soup and is not good for much. So now, add more dirt to the mix.

Now you should have mud.

How Mud Acts

The dirt under trees and flowers is good for making mud. It may even be mud already. You might find good dirt by the bank of a stream. This dirt comes already mixed with water, too.

The oldest kinds of bricks were made with mud. They were made by drying the right kind of mud. The bricks dried in the sun or over a fire. The mud baked and became hard. The right kind of mud must be used for this. Sometimes people would add straw to the mud, too. The bricks made from baked mud were sometimes called adobe.

237

In some ways, mud acts like water. In some ways, mud acts like bricks.

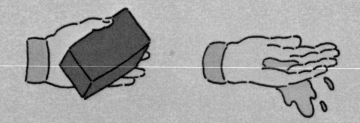

You can lift a brick with your hand.

You cannot lift water with your hand, at least not very well.

How about mud?

You can pour water from a glass.

You cannot pour a brick from a glass.

How about mud?

You can throw a brick very easily.

You cannot throw water very easily. You must use a hose or a cup or something to throw water.

How about mud?

You can count bricks.

You cannot count water.

How about mud?

You can make a pile of bricks.

You cannot make a pile of water.

How about mud?

There are lots of ways that mud isn't like bricks or like water. You cannot squish water through your fingers. It won't stay in your hand long enough. You cannot squish a brick through your fingers. It is too hard. You can easily squish mud through your fingers. It oozes slowly, and sometimes it goes *gloop* on the ground.

If you drop a brick on the ground, it bangs or clunks. Then it lies still, all in one piece. But when a brick is dropped from high up, it may break into pieces.

If you drop water on the ground, it splashes and spreads all over. But if you drop mud on the ground, it plops and splatters. Then it stands shaking in little piles.

MUD!

You cannot paint a sign with water. It has no color and just makes things wet. You cannot paint a sign with a brick because it is too hard. Its color does not come off. But you can paint a sign with mud. It is a good thing to do, too.

Bricks don't make things dirty. Sometimes, of course, bricks are already dirty. But that's not the same thing.

Water makes things wet. But it doesn't get things dirty. Water used with soap can even get things clean.

If you want to make something really dirty, just use mud!

241

MATH READING: What's It All About?

In the last story, you read about mud. Now Caroline wants to make some mud. She wants to keep track of how much mud she makes. The next page will help her.

TAKE A FIRST LOOK

Look at the next page. A graph is on the page. The graph is a special kind of graph. It is called a bar graph. What kind of book could this page come from?

FIND THE KEY IDEAS

Look at the numbers at the left. They tell how much mud Caroline made. Look under each bar. A day is written under each bar. The bar shows how much mud Caroline made on that day.

READ CAREFULLY

Now read the story on the next page. Look at the bar graph closely, too. On which day did Caroline make the most mud? On which day did Caroline make the least mud? How much mud did Caroline make on Day 2? On which day did Caroline make three cups of mud?

MAKING MUD

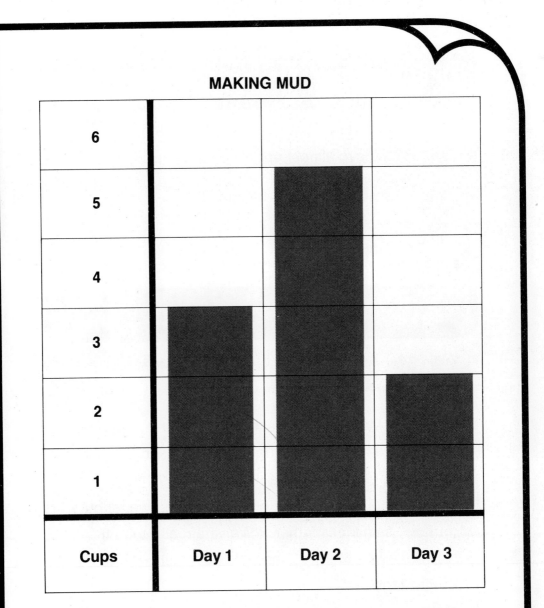

| Cups | Day 1 | Day 2 | Day 3 |

Caroline made a lot of mud. On Day 1, she made three cups of mud. On Day 2, she made five cups. On Day 3, she was tired and could make only two cups. This bar graph shows how much mud she made each day.

CHECKPOINT

Write *S* if the words have almost the same meaning. Write *O* if the words have almost opposite meanings.

1. fling—throw   **2.** clean—dirty

3. smooth—rough   **4.** town—village

5. maybe—perhaps   **6.** more—less

Write *real* if the story is true. Write *make-believe* if the story is not true.

7. Mel the Machine squeaked across the room to his parents. "I have some rough spots that squeak," he said. "Will you pour oil on the spots, please?" Neither of his parents could find the oil. " Perhaps we should try butter," said Mel's father. "We've already tried that once before," said Mel's mother. "You'll just have to squeak today, Mel."

8. There are two kinds of water on Earth. One kind is salt water. Seas and oceans are salt water. The other kind of water is fresh water. Rivers and ponds are fresh water. You can easily tell if water is salt water or fresh water. Salt water tastes salty, and fresh water does not taste salty.

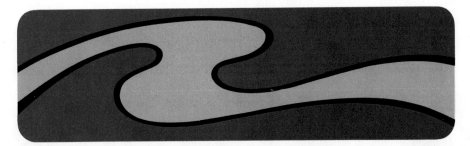

Write the best answer to each question.

Decoding:
Suffixes
-ful, -less

9. Tony was awake all night. What kind of night did Tony have?

   a. sleeping

   b. sleepless

   c. asleep

10. Beth's shirt was blue, green, and yellow. What kind of shirt did Beth have?

   a. colorless

   b. uncolored

   c. colorful

11. The beach was different every time we went back. What was the beach like?

   a. unchanged

   b. changeless

   c. changing

12. Larry couldn't sit still. How did Larry feel?

   a. restless

   b. restful

   c. resting

KUMI AND THE PEARL

Patricia Miles Martin

247

248

Kumi stood on the quay at her grandfather's pearl farm. She watched the diving girls.

Momo, her small sister, stirred against her back.

More than anything, Kumi wished that Momo could walk. Until Momo walked, Kumi could not be a diving girl. She could not hunt for oysters in the sea.

She talked to her grandfather about it. "Please, Ojii-chan, when can I be a diving girl?"

Grandfather sighed. "You may dive when Momo can walk. I will teach you to dive as I taught you to swim. You have much to learn before you can dive for oysters. You will learn to hold your breath under water. When Momo can walk, I will teach you. Until then, you will care for your small sister."

250

Kumi sighed. This she must do for her family. Her mother made kimonos for people who came to see the pearl farm. Her father and brothers worked in the sheds, helping Grandfather. There was no one else to care for Momo.

Today, Kumi looked for her friend Yukiko. Yukiko was not in the sheds. She was not on the quay watching the girls. Kumi would watch alone. She would watch with Momo sleeping against her back.

Now and then, a face pushed up through the water. An arm emptied a net full of oysters into a tub. At times a hand tucked in a strand of hair. The hair was pulled back into a knot at the back of the neck. It was the beautiful knot of shining hair worn by the diving girls.

Thoughtfully, Kumi touched her own long hair.

There was splashing and laughing in the water. No one in all Japan was happier than a diving girl. Perhaps Momo would walk soon. Perhaps she would walk tonight, at home.

When Kumi reached home, she said, " I have returned."

Her mother looked up and smiled.

Kumi unwrapped the scarf that held Momo. Carefully, she set Momo on her feet and held her.

"Walk, Momo," she whispered. "Walk."

Kumi moved her hands away. Momo's fat legs folded and she sat on the floor. It is not yet time, Kumi thought.

She started a fire and waited for the coals to grow gray. Grandfather and her father and brothers came home to eat.

After eating, Grandfather looked outside.

"We will walk. We will enjoy the beauty that is here for us to see," he said.

They walked and saw the things that were beautiful. They saw the moon, like a thin pearl hanging on a string of stars. They saw branches of cedar that seemed to brush the sky.

They came to the bank of a tumbling river. They climbed a path beside it. On they went, around a curve where the river widened. Finally they came to a deep small pool.

"It is here that I learned to dive," Kumi's mother said.

Grandfather nodded. "The pool is deep. It is almost as deep as the water at the farm."

Kumi touched her mother's sleeve. "When you were a small girl, how did you learn to stay under water? How did you know when you could dive for oysters?"

"Your grandfather taught me," her mother said. "He taught me as he will teach you, when the time comes. I remember so well. I counted the seconds each time I was in the water. One, two, three, and on to sixty. I measured them slowly, one count for each second of time. I counted until finally there was one minute."

The next morning Kumi wrapped Momo against her back. She walked along the short streets. She walked past the pearl farm and turned to climb the hill. She walked beside the river, on and on. She came to the quiet, deep pool.

Far below, she could see the pearl farm. She saw the shed where girls worked. They opened oyster shells and placed a piece of shell inside. They closed the shell again. That little piece of shell might grow into a pearl.

258

Grandfather looked small. He walked along the quay, stopping now and then.

Kumi looked down into the clear pool of green water. The water would be cold—cold from the snows of the mountains.

She turned from the pool and walked until she came to a peach tree. Something stirred in the branches. There was Yukiko perched in the tree. Quickly Yukiko slid to the ground. She reached for Momo.

"Let me carry her," she said.

"If you carry her, I will dive in the pool," Kumi said. "Then I will watch her while you dive."

"I will care for her," Yukiko said. "I don't like cold water in my ears."

Yukiko and Momo laughed together.

Kumi slipped into the water.

Down she went, forcing herself on. She felt the stones slick against her feet. Gently she bounced there like a ball. She measured out the seconds. When she knew that she must breathe, she kicked up to the surface.

Again and again she went to the bottom of the pool. Kumi rocked and balanced to keep from floating upward. She counted, one . . . two . . . three . . . and on to ten. NOW UP! She climbed out and sat on a rock to dry.

Every morning, Kumi and Momo met Yukiko. Each day Kumi dove into the pool. Each day she stayed a few seconds longer. And Momo and Yukiko played in the sunshine.

When they arrived at the pearl farm, Grandfather looked at them fondly. "They are always together, those three," he said.

"They are friends," Yukiko's father said. "One will do nothing without the other."

Then came the time when Kumi could stay under water a long time. She could stay there for almost a minute. "One more day. One more day," she thought to herself. "Perhaps tomorrow I will count to sixty . . ."

Early the next morning she began once more. Again and again, she went into the water. She stayed under water a minute, every time! What a wonderful surprise this would be for Grandfather! She sat on the bank and hugged her knees.

At the end of the day, Kumi walked back with Momo. The late afternoon grew overcast. She walked to the top of the hill. There the wind blew hard, almost as though a storm might be coming.

In the distance, Grandfather worked alone on the quay.

The wind blew with fresh, fierce force. As she watched, Grandfather slipped into the water. His arms spread wide on the floats. He didn't move—he, who could swim better than anyone—

No one hurried to help him. No one was there to help . . .

She unwound her scarf and tied Momo close to a branch. Momo could not rock in the wind. Grandfather said that she must not leave Momo. Surely, surely, this was a time to disobey. Momo would be safe, and Grandfather was in danger. She ran, stumbling, pushing against the wind.

Kumi reached the quay. She tried to call, but the words blew away with the wind.

"My ankle is caught and I cannot move it," Grandfather said.

Kumi kicked off her clogs. She dropped into the water. Grandfather's ankle was wedged between the pier and a pole. She tugged at the pole. For one minute she struggled to free his foot. Then she pushed to the surface to breathe.

"You cannot move the pier," Grandfather said. "Go for help."

"There is only one pole to move—please." Kumi slipped down into the water. She held the pole with both hands. She twisted her body as she pulled. The minute was almost over—the pole shifted . . .

Again Kumi rose to the surface. She shook the water from her face. " One more time, Grandfather. The pole moved."

And with the next tug, Grandfather pulled himself from the water. He reached out his hand to Kumi.

"How is it that you hold your breath under water?" he asked.

"I practiced at the deep pool," Kumi said.

"And Momo?"

"Yukiko cared for her."

"And now? Where is Momo?" Grandfather asked.

"She is tied in a tree," Kumi said softly.

"I see, " Grandfather said. "I see."

Grandfather led the way up the hill. Although he limped, they climbed quickly. Momo was still sleeping in her hammock. She woke. She cried when she was wrapped against Kumi's wet back.

The next night, Grandfather began to speak.

"Tomorrow . . . I will have a new . . . diver. I have spoken to the foreman. His daughter, Yukiko, wishes . . . to care for Momo."

Kumi threw her arms around her grandfather's neck. " How can I wait until tomorrow? How can I wait?"

The next morning, she floated near her own wooden tub. A long rope tied around her waist, reached to the tub. Deep under water, she felt along the shoreline. Her fingers searched until she found an oyster. She pulled it from its ledge and kicked to the top.

"Swim here," Grandfather called. He knelt and reached for the oyster. "We will mark this one before it goes to the aging rack. When it grows a pearl, that pearl will be yours to keep."

" Please, Ojii-chan, the pearl will be for Yukiko who watches Momo."

"It shall be as you wish," Grandfather said.

That night they walked in their garden.

Clouds edged with light floated across the moon.

Proudly, Kumi tucked a strand of hair into her small knot. It was the knot of shining hair worn by the diving girls.

GLOSSARY

Full pronunciation key*   The pronunciation of each word
is shown just after the word, in this way: **ab•bre•vi•ate** (ə brē′vē āt).
    The letters and signs used are pronounced as in the words below.
    The mark ′ is placed after a syllable with primary or
heavy accent, as in the example above.
    The mark ′ after a syllable shows a secondary or lighter accent,
as in **ab•bre•vi•a•tion** (ə brē′vē ā′shən).

a	hat, cap	**k**	kind, seek	**ᵀH**	then, smooth
ā	age, face	**l**	land, coal	**u**	cup, butter
ä	father, far	**m**	me, am	**u̇**	full, put
b	bad, rob	**n**	no, in	**ü**	rule, move
ch	child, much	**ng**	long, bring		
d	did, red	**o**	hot, rock	**v**	very, save
		ō	open, go	**w**	will, woman
e	let, best	**ô**	order, all	**y**	young, yet
ē	equal, be	**oi**	oil, voice	**z**	zero, breeze
ėr	term, learn	**ou**	house, out	**zh**	measure, seizure
f	fat, if			**ə**	represents:
g	go, bag	**p**	paper, cup		a in about
h	he, how	**r**	run, try		e in taken
		s	say, yes		i in pencil
i	it, pin	**sh**	she, rush		o in lemon
ī	ice, five	**t**	tell, it		u in circus
j	jam, enjoy	**th**	thin, both		

* Pronunciation key and respellings are from *Scott, Foresman Beginning Dictionary* by E. L. Thorndike and Clarence Barnhart. Copyright © 1979 by Scott, Foresman and Company. Reprinted by permission.

A

a·bue·lo (ä bwā′lō) *Spanish* grandfather.

act (akt) 1. a division of a play: "The first *act* of the play was the best." 2. a deed. 3. to do something.

add (ad) 1. to state further. 2. to increase: "The new detective *added* more information."

al·li·ga·tor (al′ə gā′tər) a large reptile with a scaly hide and sharp teeth: "An *alligator* lives in a swamp."

al·read·y (ôl red′ē) by now: "I have *already* washed my face."

a·quar·i·um (ə kwer′ē əm) 1. a zoo for water plants, fish, and other sea animals: "We saw seals and whales at the *aquarium*." 2. a tank in which fish and water plants are kept.

at·ten·tion (ə ten′shən) 1. care; concern; consideration: "We paid *attention* to Albert on his birthday."

aunt (ant) the sister of your mother or father: "*Aunt* Sally is my mother's sister."

B

ba·by (bā′bē) 1. a young child. 2. a young animal: "The *baby* alligator came out of its egg." **babies.**

bal·loon (bə lün′) 1. a small rubber bag filled with air: "The *balloons* floated into the air." 2. a large bag filled with hot air or gas to make it rise above the ground.

be (bē) to exist or take place: "The children have *been* at home all day." **was** or **were, been, being.**

be·lieve (bi lēv′) to accept as true: "I *believe* that the lake is very deep." **believed, believing.**

big (big) 1. large: "A pony is *big,* a horse is *bigger,* and an elephant is the *biggest.*" 2. important. **bigger, biggest.** 3. grown up.

birth·day (bėrth′dā′) the day that you were born: "Albert's *birthday* is on May 13."

branch (branch) a part of a tree that grows out from the trunk:

274

"Father cut the dead *branches* from the oak tree." **branches.**

bull (bu̇l) the male of cattle, elephants, whales, or moose: "The *bull* became angry when he was chased."

bull·doz·er (bu̇l'dō'zər) a heavy tractor with a steel blade mounted in front used to move earth: "The *bulldozer* was moving large piles of dirt."

buy (bī) to purchase: "Sally will *buy* mittens for the children." **bought.**

car (kär) an automobile: "Beth drove her *car* to the store."

car·ry (kar'ē) to take something or someone from one place to another: "Jim will *carry* the dishes to the sink." **carries, carried, carrying.**

chair (cher *or* char) a seat or bench: "There were two empty *chairs* at the table."

child (chīld) a young girl or boy: "*Children* like to read funny books." **children.**

class (klas) 1. a group of students taught together: "The cartoonist drew interesting pictures for the *class*." 2. a group of people or things alike in some way. **classes.**

clean (klēn) 1. free from dirt: "Paintbrushes must be kept *clean*." 2. pure. 3. simple.

close (klōs) near; having little space between: "We moved *closer* to the teacher so that we could hear what she said." **closer, closest.**

cloth (klôth) woven fabric or material: "The dress was made of beautiful *cloth*."

clothes (klōz) things to wear: "I bought a new shirt, pants, and some other *clothes*."

clue (klü) a hint that helps to solve a mystery or problem: "The detective solved the mystery by using *clues*."

275

com·pa·ny (kum′pə nē) 1. a business group: "Many people can work for the telephone *company.*" **companies.** 2. people who come to visit.

corn (kôrn) a yellow or white grain used for food: "*Corn* is used for food for people and animals."

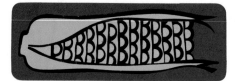

course (kôrs) 1. a way; a path; a track. 2. —**of course** (ov kôrs) surely, as expected: "The sun rises every day, *of course.*"

cry (krī) 1. a loud sound: "An excited *cry* came from the classroom." **cries.** 2. to sob. **cries, cried, crying.**

cur·tain (kėrt′n) 1. a piece of cloth hung at a window: "The wind blew the *curtains* away from the window." 2. a piece of cloth in front of a stage.

D

de·cide (di sīd′) to make up your mind: "Ana *decided* to play basketball after school." **decided, deciding.**

de·tec·tive (di tek′tiv) one who solves crimes, often working with police: "A *detective* was sent to investigate the crime."

di·al (dī′əl) 1. a flat, round disk with numbers or letters on it. 2. the face of a clock or watch. 3. the controls on a machine. 4. to make a call by means of a dial on a telephone: "Ken learned to *dial* the telephone." 5. to use a dial to choose a number or letter.

dirt (dėrt) 1. soil, earth, or mud. 2. anything that makes something unclean: "His new jeans were covered with *dirt.*"

door (dôr) a piece of wood, glass, or metal that closes off an opening to a room or building: "I opened the *door* and went into the house."

dye (dī) a substance used to color fabric and other material: "My grandmother *dyed* the curtains blue." **dyed, dyeing.**

E

ear (ir) 1. the part of some plants that contains grains: "That *ear* of corn was delicious." 2. the part of the body through which people and animals hear.

eas·i·ly (ē′zə lē) 1. without trouble: "You can *easily* write your name." 2. surely.

en·ter (en′tər) 1. to go into: "Rachel *enters* the class late every day." 2. to join.

e·ven (ē′vən) 1. as one would not expect: "The magician could *even* make water change color." 2. equal. 3. level.

F

fam·i·ly (fam′ə lē) 1. parents and their children: "My mother, father, sister, and I are the people in our *family*." 2. a group of people related by birth or marriage. **families.**

farm·er (fär′mər) a person who raises animals and crops: "The *farmer* raised large turkeys."

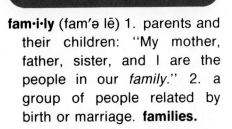

fa·ther (fä′ᴛʜər) a male parent: "My *father* helped me read the recipe."

fin·ger (fing′gər) one of the five end parts of the hand: "Ann's *fingers* were too big for her mitten."

flow·er (flou′ər) a blossom; a part of a plant: "Roses are a kind of *flower*."

fool·ish (fü′lish) silly; senseless: "*Foolish* cartoons often make children laugh."

foot (füt) 1. part of the body that extends from the end of the leg: "The baby stood on its *feet* and took a step." 2. a unit of measure equal to twelve inches. **feet.**

front (frunt) the opposite of back: "A tree grew in the *front* yard."

full (fül) complete; can hold no more: "The gas tank was completely *full*."

fun·ny (fun′ē) 1. making you laugh: "I laughed at the *funny* joke." 2. odd. **funnier, funniest.**

G

gar·den (gärd′n) a piece of land where plants, flowers, or vegetables are grown: "Carlos grew corn and potatoes in his *garden*."

give (giv) 1. to hand over as a gift: "Jan is *giving* Jim a surprise party." 2. to pay. 3. to yield to force. **gave, given, giving.**

grand·fa·ther (grand′fä′ŦHər) a parent's father: "Carmen's *grandfather* writes stories for the newspaper."

grand·moth·er (grand′muŦH′ər) a parent's mother: "My *grandmother* is a good storyteller."

grand·son (grand′sun′) the son of one's son or daughter: "Ted gave his *grandson* a lot of attention."

gro·cer·y (grō′sər ē) 1. a store that sells food and household items: "I went to the *grocery* to buy some milk." 2. articles of food. **groceries.**

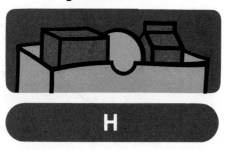

hair (her *or* har) the mass of threadlike growth from the top of the head: "Her brown *hair* was very curly."

hi·ja (ē′hä) *Sp.* daughter.

hi·jo (ē′hō) *Sp.* son.

hur·ri·cane (hėr′ə kān) a storm with very strong winds and heavy rain: "The *hurricane* blew down trees and soaked the land."

I

im·por·tant (im pôrt′nt) having meaning; value: "It is so *important* to look before you cross the street."

in·ter·est (in′tər ist) concern or desire to know: "Parents are *interested* in their children."

K

ker·nel (kėr′nl) 1. a grain or seed of wheat or corn: "Each *kernel* of corn was deep yellow." 2. an important part of anything.

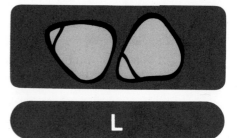

lamb (lam) a young sheep: "The *lamb* cried for its mother."

large (lärj) big in size; huge: "A *large* group watched our play."

less (les) 1. smaller. 2. not as much: "It was *less* rainy today than on Monday."

les·son (les'n) something to be learned or taught: "Dan had a music *lesson* after school."

li·on (lī'ən) a large, yellow cat with a shaggy mane, found in Africa: "The *lion* is sometimes called the king of the jungle."

love·ly (luv'lē) 1. pretty. 2. delightful: "The tailor made a *lovely* suit." **lovelier, loveliest.**

M

ma·chine (mə shēn') a device whose parts work together to get a job done, for example, a sewing machine: "A lawn mower is a useful *machine.*"

mail (māl) 1. letters, cards, and packages sent through a postal system: "There was a letter from my cousin in today's *mail.*" 2. to send letters, cards, and packages through a postal system.

main (mān) 1. chief; most important: "Elizabeth had the *main* part in the class play." 2. a large pipe that carries water, gas, or sewage.

mark (märk) 1. a spot or line: "Wild animals make interesting *marks* in the dirt." 2. a grade to show how well one has done.

mar·ket (mär'kit) an open area or a building where food, clothes, or other things are sold: "The farmers sold their corn at the *market.*"

mi (mē) *Sp.* my.

milk (milk) a white liquid from a cow, used for drinking and cooking: "Our family drinks a lot of *milk.*"

mit·ten (mit'n) a warm covering for the hand with one part for four fingers and the other part for the thumb: "Lin took off one *mitten* to pick up her pencil."

move (müv) 1. to go from one place to another: "The sailboat was *moving* across the lake." 2. to cause to change place. 3. to go to another place to live. **moved, moving.**

279

mys·ter·i·ous (mi stir′ē əs) hard to explain: "The movie was *mysterious* and scary."

N

na·ture (nā′chər) all things in the world not made by people: "Rainbows are one of the wonders of *nature*."

nei·ther (nē′ℸHər *or* nī′ℸHər) not either: "*Neither* boat is wet."

O

o·cean (ō′shən) the large body of salt water that covers much of the earth: "The ship sailed across the *ocean* from one country to another."

op·e·ra·tor (op′ə rā′tər) a person who makes something work, for example, a machine: "The telephone *operator* will help you if you can't dial a number."

P

page (pāj) a side of a sheet of paper: "The picture of the lion is on *page* ten."

paint·er (pān′tər) 1. an artist; one who paints pictures: "The *painter* made a picture of a sunset." 2. a person who paints houses.

par·ent (per′ənt *or* par′ənt) a father or mother: "Her *parents* are happy with just one child."

part (pärt) 1. one section of something: "What *part* of the book did you like the best?" 2. a share.

par·ty (pär′tē) a group of people having a good time together: "I love to go to birthday *parties*!" **parties.**

pea·cock (pē′kok′) a large male bird with colorful tail feathers of green, blue, and gold: "The *peacock* spread out his beautiful tail."

per·haps (pər haps′) maybe: "*Perhaps* tomorrow will be a sunny day."

pick·le (pik′əl) 1. certain kinds of vegetables, such as beets or cucumbers, preserved in brine: "*Pickles* taste good on sandwiches." 2. trouble.

pic·ture (pik'chər) a painting or drawing: "We drew *pictures* of our class trip."

plate (plāt) 1. a round dish used to place food on. 2. in baseball, a flat rubber marker at which the batter stands: "Elizabeth stepped up to the *plate* with her bat in her hand."

pour (pôr) to cause to flow: "*Pour* the milk carefully into the glass."

pow·der (pou'dər) a substance made up of fine particles formed by pounding a solid material: "Baking *powder* is needed to make a cake."

pre·tend (pri tend') to make believe: "The young child closed her eyes and *pretended* to be asleep."

pun·ish (pun'ish) to cause loss or pain in some way for doing something wrong: "Elizabeth was *punished* for playing with matches."

purr (pėr) to make a low sound as a cat does when it is happy: "Jack petted the cat, and it started to *purr*."

purse (pėrs) a small bag or pocketbook in which to carry money and other things: "The *purse* had some coins and a pen in it."

ques·tion (kwes'chən) 1. something that asks for information: "The children asked the teacher many *questions* about the lesson." 2. doubt.

quite (kwīt) very; really: "It is *quite* hot today."

R

rec·i·pe (res'ə pē) a set of directions for preparing something, usually food: "This *recipe* for soup is hard to follow."

re·mem·ber (ri mem'bər) 1. to recall; to think of again: "I can't *remember* where I put my books." 2. to not forget.

rid·dle (rid'l) a puzzle: "*Riddles* can be hard to figure out."

281

riv·er (riv′ər) a stream of water that empties into a body of water, such as a lake, pond, or ocean: "The *river* flowed into the sea."

rough (ruf) 1. stormy: "The *rough* water made the ship roll." 2. tough in manner. 3. coarse. **rougher, roughest.**

rub·ber (rub′ər) a stretchy material made from the sap of a tree or in a laboratory: "Tires are made of *rubber*."

S

sad (sad) unhappy: "*Sadly* she waved good-by to her friend." **sadder, saddest. —sadly.**

seal (sēl) a sea animal with large flippers, usually found in cold areas: "We saw a *seal* swimming in the ocean."

se·cret (sē′krit) information that is kept from others: "He wouldn't tell me his *secret*."

sell (sel) to give something in return for money: "We *sold* our house when we moved to a new city." **sold, selling.**

shirt (shėrt) a piece of clothing worn on the upper part of the body: "He pulled his *shirt* on over his head."

silk (silk) 1. a soft thread made by a kind of caterpillar called a silkworm. 2. cloth made from silk thread. 3. the shiny tassles under the husk of an ear of corn: "He took the corn *silk* off before cooking the corn."

smile (smīl) 1. to grin: "Sara *smiled* when she saw her friend." **smiled, smiling.** 2. a pleasant look on your face:

solve (solv) to find an answer to: "Has the detective *solved* the mystery yet?" **solved, solving.**

son (sun) a male child: "Mr. Stone said his *son* was at school."

speed (spēd) fast movement: "The *speed* of a flying airplane is greater than that of a flying bird."

stalk (stôk) 1. the main stem of a plant: "The *stalk* of the flower had been broken." 2. to pursue without being seen or heard.

stat·ue (stach′ü) a solid model of someone or something made of wood, stone, clay, or metal:

"There was a big stone *statue* of a whale near the door to the aquarium."

storm (stôrm) a state of weather with strong wind and rain, snow, hail, thunder, or lightning: "The *storm* brought two feet of snow and high winds."

sto·ry (stôr'ē) 1. a real or make-believe telling of an event or happening; a tale: "Authors write *stories* for books." 2. one floor in a building. **stories.**

sug·ar (shug'ər) a sweet substance made from sugar cane or sugar beets: "Many cereals are full of *sugar.*"

suit (süt) a set of clothes that go together, such as pants and jacket or skirt and jacket: "Mother wore her new *suit* to the office."

sum·mer (sum'ər) the time of year that comes after spring and before fall: "*Summer* is the hottest time of year."

switch (swich) 1. something that makes or breaks an electrical connection. 2. to change or turn: "The traffic light *switches* from green to red and back to green." **switches.**

T

ta·ble (tā'bəl) a flat piece of furniture with legs below: "Our kitchen *table* has a round top and four legs."

tai·lor (tā'lər) a person whose business it is to fix or make clothes: "The *tailor* made a fine-looking suit."

taste (tāst) 1. the ability to tell whether something is sweet, sour, salty, or bitter: "Let's *taste* the pie to see if we like it." 2. a personal dislike. **tasted, tasting.**

tel·e·phone (tel'ə fōn) 1. an instrument used to send sound over wires: "Emily grabbed the *telephone* to call the fire station." 2. to use the telephone to call someone. **telephoned, telephoning.**

throw (thrō) 1. to toss into the air. 2. to project; to send out: "*Throw* the baseball to the pitcher." **threw, thrown, throwing.**

tip·toe (tip'tō') 1. to walk on the tips of one's toes: "Tony

283

tiptoes past the sleeping dog." 2. the tips of one's toes. **tiptoed, tiptoeing.**

to·geth·er (tə geŦH′ər) with each other: "The children were standing *together*."

touch (tuch) to feel: "You will hurt your hand if you *touch* the hot stove." **touches.**

trap (trap) 1. something used to catch animals: "Ann set a *trap* to catch the crabs." 2. to catch something off guard. **trapped, trapping.**

try (trī) 1. to make an attempt at: "Dave *tried* to hit the baseball." 2. to test. **tries, tried, trying.**

tu·na (tü′nə) a large salt water fish that is used for food: "*Tuna* are very large fish."

tur·key (tėr′kē) a large North American bird, now bred for its meat: "A *turkey* is much bigger than a chicken."

tur·nip (tėr′nəp) the large, roundish root of a plant eaten as a vegetable: "*Turnip* can be eaten raw or cooked."

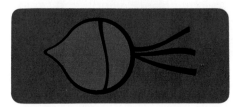

twelve (twelv) the number after eleven and before thirteen; 12: "*Twelve* o'clock is one hour later than eleven o'clock."

U

ug·ly (ug′lē) 1. unattractive to look at; homely: "The peacock is not an *ugly* bird." 2. cranky. **uglier, ugliest.**

un·til (un til′) up to the time of: "We waited *until* morning for the sun to rise."

u·pon (ə pôn′) on: "I climbed *upon* a stool to reach the shelf."

V

va·ca·tion (vā kā′shən) a period when one does not work or go to school: "Summer *vacation* is a favorite time for students."

vain (vān) 1. proud, boastful: "The *vain* boy was always combing his hair." 2. unsuccessful.

vil·lage (vil′ij) a group of homes smaller than a town: "We sailed our boat to a small fishing *village*."

vis·it (viz′it) to go to see: "We will *visit* grandmother today."

W

warm (wôrm) having some heat; more hot than cold: "The summer night was still *warm* from the sun's heat."

wash (wosh) to clean with water: "*Wash* your hands in the sink before dinner." **washes.**

watch (woch) 1. to guard: "The guard *watched* throughout the long night." 2. to look at. **watches.**

weath·er (weŦH′ər) the state of the air at a certain time and place: "The *weather* can be hot and dry in the South."

weigh (wā) to find out how heavy something is: "An elephant *weighs* a lot."

whis·per (hwis′pər) 1. to speak very low and softly: "The teacher asked the children to *whisper* quietly." 2. a low, soft sound.

wob·ble (wob′əl) to rock from side to side: "The *wobbly* chair tipped over when I sat on it." **wobbled, wobbling. —wobbly.**

won·der (wun′dər) to wish to know something: "Beth Ann *wondered* where her dog was."

wool (wu̇l) the soft curly hair of sheep and other animals that is used to make fabric: "A *wool* suit is very warm."

work·er (wėr′kər) someone who works: "The *workers* were tired after their long day making cars."

worm (wėrm) a small, thin, creeping animal with a soft body: "*Worms* live under the ground."

wor·ry (wėr′ē) to feel concern or be upset: "Don't *worry* about the broken dish." **worries, worried, worrying.**

wrong (rông) incorrect; the opposite of right: "Lou wrote the *wrong* answer on the paper."

(Acknowledgments continued from page 2)

Dietz and Harry Goodridge. Used by permission of the publisher.

Lothrop, Lee & Shepard Company for "Feather in the Wind," abridged and adapted from *Feather in the Wind* (without illustrations) by Doris Van Liew Foster. Text Copyright © 1972 by Doris Van Liew Foster. By permission of Lothrop, Lee & Shepard Company (A Division of William Morrow & Company). Also for the adaptation of *Pea Soup and Sea Serpents* (without illustrations) by William E. Schroder. Copyright © 1977 by William E. Schroder. By permission of Lothrop, Lee & Shepard Company (A Division of William Morrow & Company).

Lilian Moore for "Go With the Poem" from her book *Go With the Poem*. Copyright © 1979 by Lilian Moore. Reprinted with permission of the author.

Oxford University Press, England, for "Anansi Finds a Fool" retold by Verna Aardema. Adapted from *Akan-Ashanti Folk-Tales* by R. S. Rattray (1930) by permission of Oxford University Press.

Scholastic Inc. for "What the Wind Told," an adaptation of excerpts from *What the Wind Told* by Betty Boegehold. Text copyright © 1974 by Betty Boegehold. Reprinted by permission of Four Winds Press, a division of Scholastic Inc.

Millicent Selsam for the abridged, adapted text of her book *How to Be a Nature Detective*. Text copyright © 1958, 1963 by Millicent Selsam. Used by permission of the author.

Toni Strassman for the poem "Written in Sand" from *We Walk in Sandy Places* by Byrd Baylor. Text copyright by Byrd Baylor 1976. By permission of Toni Strassman, Agent. Published by Charles Scribner's Sons.

Illustrators and Photographers: Peter Bradford, cover, 8-9, 66-67, 124-125, 184-185; Shane Kelley, 1, 3-7, 32-33, 40-41, 50-51, 64-65, 84-85, 94-95, 104-105, 122-123, 152-155, 162-163, 182-183, 204-205, 216-217, 242-245; Kevin Young, 8-9, 66-67, 124-125, 184-185; Carolyn McHenry, 10-17, 34-39, 146-151, 197-203; Tomie dePaola 18-31; Jack Kent, 42-49; Stephen Ogilvy, 52-55; David McCall Johnston, 56-57; Susanna Natti, 58-63; Gary Fujiwara, 68, 207-213; Robert Tallon, 69-75; Michael L. Pateman, 76-83, 172-181; Dorothea Sierra, 86-93, 126-133; Patrick Blackwell, 96-103, 228-241; Maxie Chambliss, 106-111; Jerry Pinkney, 112-121, 139-145; Lucinda McQueen, 134-138; Barbara Osborne, 156; Aliki, 157-161; Janina Domanska, 164-171; Reprinted by permission of Coward, McCann & Geoghegan, Inc. from *Nate the Great and the Lost List* by Marjorie Weinman Sharmat. Illustrations copyright © 1975 by Marc Simont, 186-196; Robert Froman, 206; Stephen G. Maka, 214-215; Kristen Dietrich, 218; William Schroder, 219-227; Steven Masami Takenaga, 246-272; William McDade, 273-285.

Design, Ginn Reading Program:
Creative Director: Peter Bradford
Art Director: Gary Fujiwara
Design Coordinator: Anne Todd
Design: Lorraine Johnson, Linda Post, Kevin Young, Cathy Bennett, Kristen Dietrich

286

CDEFGHIJO876543
Printed in the United States of America